# FOR SUCH A TIME AS THIS

## THE STORY OF MARY MATHEWS

Benny Varghese

**OPEN DOOR**
Publications Pvt. Ltd.

ISBN: 978-81-924647-5-6

Distributed by Children's Network International Inc.
(CNI) 5449 Robin Hill Court, Norcross, GA 30093
Email contact: thampymat@gmail.com

*For further information about Mary Mathews and
Ministry write to us:*
Email: paul@nmmindia.org

*I dedicate this book to all the women who have made an indelible impression of commitment and missionary sacrifice through their unceasing toil for the expansion of the Kingdom of God.*

# Contents

Foreword .................................................................................. 5

Greetings ............................................................................... 7

Introduction .......................................................................... 9

Reflections from Home .................................................... 13

A Macedonian Call ............................................................ 17

Setting Foot in Udaipur ................................................... 21

Not By Sight But By Faith ............................................... 25

Hand of God Revealed in the Last Hour .................... 29

Amazing Grace .................................................................... 33

God's Glory and Provision in the Desert .................... 37

Manohar Bhawan at Chetak Circle ............................. 41

An Inheritance Among the Natives .............................. 45

He Will Command His Angels ....................................... 47

Miracles of Healing Wrought Through Prayers ........ 51

Light in the Darkness ....................................................... 55

Evolution of a Woman Missionary ............................... 59

Even the Buildings Praise ............................................... 63

A Door That No One Can Shut ..................................... 69

Imprints of Courage .......................................................... 75

Manifestation of an Awakening .................................... 83

Navapur Convention: A Small Beginning .................. 89

To Love, Cherish and Obey ............................................ 95

Passing the Baton ............................................................... 99

The Next Stage .................................................................. 105

An Interview with Mrs. Mary Mathews ..................... 108

References ........................................................................... 112

**Rev. Dr. K. C. John**

# FOREWORD

The writer of the biography of Mary Mathews titled "For Such A Time As This," has in a blessed manner accomplished a commendable work with rich content.

Dr. Thomas Mathews was an important person amongst the pioneer missionaries with apostolic vision, who went from Kerala to North India for ministry.

Half a century ago, Dr. Thomas Mathews came to Rajasthan, which was a place with more difficult and harsh conditions than now, and made it the centre of his ministry activities. He emerged victorious, flying the gospel flag high in Udaipur and conquering the conditions that prevailed there. Mrs. Mary Mathews is the beloved wife of that great servant of God.

This book is the portrayal of the life experiences of this great lady, who shared the life of Dr. Thomas Mathews and the call of God on him.

Mrs. Mary Mathews, without allowing her heart to waver, has overcome heart-breaking sorrows and ferociously adverse conditions. She dedicated herself to her beloved husband, whom she loved as much as her own life, and above all, to Jesus Christ, whom she loved more than her own life. This commitment, which has become a model for thousands, is revealed in the biography of Mrs. Mary Mathews that will make the readers long to do the gospel work.

Especially, the creative style of the author Pastor Benny Varghese in presenting the biography that provides reading pleasure is notable and admirable.

The harvest in North India is ripe and is waiting for missionaries to reap it. It is a need of the hour that thousands of sincere and dedicated people from this generation come forward and rise to be part of missionary activities.

"The harvest truly is plentiful, but the labourers are few. Therefore pray the Lord of the harvest to send out labourers into His harvest." Matthew 9:37, 38 (NKJV).

This book is an invitation for the accomplishment of these words of Jesus Christ.

All those who love the gospel should buy and read a copy of this book, which is being published in three languages.

I pray that our great God will continue to bless Sister Mary Mathews, her family members and co-workers in their current missionary activities.


I express all my best wishes.

**Rev. Dr. K. C. John**
**General Secretary: Indian Pentecostal Church of God**
**Chairman: Power Vision Telecasting Co. Ltd.**

**Sis. Aleyamma Varughese**

# GREETINGS

*"King's daughters are among Your honorable women"*
Psalm 45:9 (NKJV)

When I was offered the opportunity to write a few lines in the pages of the biography on Mrs. Mary Mathews, the above verse of the Bible readily came to my mind. Having read the draft version of this book, I know this verse is apt for her.

I experienced the humbleness, nobleness and God fearing nature of beloved Mary Mathews during the short time we interacted with each other.

Bearing the sorrow of the loss of her mother at an innocent age in her childhood, when Mary was studying in the 10th standard, God spoke to her through His prophet. As she heard the prophecy, she submitted herself to God for ministry to North India according to God's guidance.

In God's time, according to His plans, she got married to Dr. Thomas Mathews and reached Udaipur in Rajasthan and became God's witness.

God used her for the salvation of thousands. While giving birth to three children, she became a mother to thousands of depressed and orphaned women and children. She transformed many underprivileged and led many from spiritual darkness to God's divine light.

God showered grace on her and gave her the potential to stand in the places where God appointed her. Faithfully serving God, her husband, Pastor Mathews completed his mission in this world and went to his heavenly abode.

Even while suffering the grief inflicted by the departure of her beloved husband, God gave her abundant grace to take over the burden of the ministry entrusted by God and put her personal touch to it.

God has personally blessed me by providing an opportunity to visit Udaipur and to understand the mininstry going on there.

With due respects and regards I pray that this biography of Mrs. Mary Mathews will be a blessing for many more women in and out of India. May this be an adornment on sister Mary Mathews.

Exactly like the verse in the Bible, "They shall still bear fruit in old age; they shall be fresh and flourishing" Psalm 92:14 (NJKV), may sister Mary Mathews be a channel of relief and blessing to many. I pray that may the name of God attain eminence through her.

May God honour Pastor Benny Varghese, who ventured to create a book that is capable of encouraging many spiritually.

May his blessed pen give birth to many more valuable creations.


Best wishes and prayers,

**Sis. Aleyamma Varughese**
**(W/o Rev. Dr. M.A. Varughese)**
**Bethel AG Church**
**Bangalore**

# INTRODUCTION

"Lives of great men all remind us, we can make our lives sublime, and, departing, leave behind us, footprints on the sands of time." - H. W. Longfellow.

The most special attribute of a biographic work is that it enables us to read within a few hours an account of the experiences of a lifetime.

Since a biography is not a work of fiction, the places, incidents and people mentioned in it are real. Sometimes, we might experience that we are encountering these people at various phases as we read the book. If not all, I believe that at least some pages of this book will speak to you and touch you.

Had Mary Mathews reached north India only because of her marriage to Dr. Thomas Mathews, one of the most eminent Christian leaders India has ever seen, and remained a mere shadow, this book would have been meaningless.

Even before her marriage, she had received the call and vision from God for North India. In other words, Mary had, in her teenage years, got a clear picture about what her commission from God was and where her work lay.

That was a significant day in her childhood, when God spoke to her through His prophet, He had promised "You too will be a mother to thousands. Many will call you, 'Mother'!"

This promise has evidently been fulfilled in Mary's life. We can understand it from the words of Glory, the daughter of Mary Mathews: "When we were young mummy's desire used to be that she would have enough money so that she could give to people who came asking for help. Mummy always cared to give food and fare to anyone coming anytime. If someone in financially dire straits visited, she would always have money to bless the needy."

A mentionable trait in her character is her exceptional ability to maintain her composure in conflict-ridden circumstances. People who generally suppress anger, stress, frustrations and emotions inside may ultimately explode in emotional outbursts when tension builds up or exceeds the level of endurance. But her daughter Glory and son-in-law Finny Philip unanimously testify: "Whatever may be the popular opinion, we haven't seen mummy giving into emotional outburst, even once, despite enduring hunger, deprivations and hardships. We have never heard her complaining, murmuring, or reacting all these years."

It was from Mary that girls, who had come from remote hamlets to study in the Filadelfia Bible College in Udaipur, learnt all aspects of hospitality including the primary lessons. The incidents of those girls going back after learning many practical things like the 'art of kitchen management' which are outside the ambit of the Bible college syllabus and holding the helm of well managed conventions in villages have become common today.

The social, cultural and spiritual movements Mary and her team initiated and led among the semi-naked and primitive *adivasi* tribal women have now become part of history. Today, they have learnt to drape sarees well and live with dignity.

Mary has been a motivation in uplifting women and bringing them to the mainstream of the society. The honour of being the first Indian woman to drive a scooter in Udaipur also goes to her.

Possessing faith as the only asset, she has come thus far. It is not an exaggeration to describe Mary Mathews as a woman of great faith. It was the time when the Bible school building was being constructed in Udaipur – perhaps, it was then that they faced the largest financial challenge ever. One of those days, Mary happened to see a vision. She saw the word 'Jesus' written in tiny letters; it was just readable size. She then saw each of the letters of the word gradually emerging bigger and finally, the word covering the whole Filadelfia campus. Mary immediately grasped the meaning of the vision – that Jesus is sufficient for all. And this has stuck with her all this while.

The main purpose behind writing this book is to motivate the women to dream big for God. If this book encourages them to a certain extent just to realize their relevance and role in missionary activities in church, in family and in society, I will consider myself blessed in Christ.

I do not claim that this book is complete or faultless. Maybe many more events, places and people should have been mentioned in this book. The sacrifices or contributions of any individual are not belittled merely for the reason that they are not mentioned in this book. Your righteousness, labour and sacrifice are not vain in Christ, on the other hand, they are invaluable.

"Let the one who does wrong continue to do wrong; let the vile person continue to be vile; let the one who does right continue to do right; and let the holy person continue to be holy. Look, I am coming soon! My reward is with me, and I will give to each person according to what they have done (Revelation 22: 11, 12)".

I am greatly indebted to the many individuals who have inspired and helped me author this book. It is impossible to mention all the names, but I would like to highlight a few of them. I am very grateful to Rev.Dr. K.C. John and Smt. Aleyamma Varughese for their words, which have added fragrance to this book. I am extremely thankful to Rev. Dr. Paul Mathews for all his help in the publication of this book.

I thank God for one and all who prayed for me and helped me. The responsibility of faults in this book lies with me while all glory goes to the Lord Jesus Christ.

With the prayer that hundreds of sisters taking a leaf out of dear Mary Aunty's book, will rise from the land of India to contribute to the expansion and glorification of the Kingdom of God, I humbly present this book before the esteemed readers.

With prayer and gratitude,

**In the Lord's Vineyard,**
**Pastor Benny Varghese**

# 01

# REFLECTIONS FROM HOME

Mary was born on November 7, 1947, in the village of Koottala, located in the city of Thrissur, Kerala. She was the third child of Podimannil P. V. George and his wife Annamma. Her parents were devout Christians and deeply loved the Lord. She grew up with her parents and siblings in a farmland in the village. She was lovingly called Marykutty at home and by her close knit family members and friends.

At the age of 10, she and her family were caught up in a crucible of unspeakable sorrows when her mother suddenly fell ill and died. Growing up as a young girl, she faced hazardous realities and difficulties in the absence of her mother.

The vacuum and sorrow caused by the demise of her mother was beyond all bearing. Because both her older siblings were boys, obliging the customary practice in an average Indian household, the heartbroken ten–year–old girl had to assume charge of the home's kitchen. She also had to take care of her three younger siblings. After sending them to school, she herself had to travel on bus to attend school, eight kilometres away.

Her mother's untimely demise dealt a huge blow to Mary's faith.

Though she was born and brought up in a Christian family that maintained high spiritual standards, and had gained the born again experience at a very young age, when confronted with the harsh realities of life she could not but question God, her Creator. The God she had been acquainted with in the Bible was the embodiment of love and benevolence.

"Is this the love of God? Is this how He loves? My father is a very devout man. My mother was extremely pious. If there were any mistakes or faults, couldn't God have corrected them? Would a loving God punish so cruelly? These questions often raced through Mary's young mind.

She constantly questioned the Word of God. As she grew disenchanted with life, faith gave way to frustration, the fear of God was lost and spiritual interest waned. Only because she feared her devout father, she used to attend the Sunday worship services.

Some more years passed by and Mary was now studying in the 10th grade in school. The bruises caused by the demise of her mother remained unhealed in her heart. This time around, a servant of God known as Mosha *Upadeshi* (a pastor or an evangelist was called by the title *Upadeshi* implying spiritual advisor or teacher) had been travelling in and around Koottala village conducting spiritual revival meetings.

Mary's father decided to conduct a prayer meeting with this pastor during the day at his house. But Mary did not want to attend. To skip this gathering, she left for school much earlier than usual. She waited at the bus stop for the 8 am bus; but that bus did not show up even after waiting for a long time. On Pattikkad – Thrissur route, buses ply with a frequency of one bus every 20 to 30 minutes, but that day, she waited till 11am and not a single bus turned up. She was left with no other option but to return to her house where the prayer meeting was on.

## Chapter 01

Meanwhile, as scheduled, the prayer meeting was in progress at her house. She was walking back at a very slow pace hoping that the meeting would end before she reached home. But, despite walking as slow as possible, the meeting was far from being over when she entered the premises of the house. She quietly crept in from the backdoor and sat in the farthest corner of the room where nobody could see her.

It came unexpected and suddenly! Mosha *Upadeshi* walked through the gathered people towards the end and laying his hand on the head of Marykutty emphatically prophesied God's message: "My dear daughter! Have you been angry with me over the death of your mother? I took back your mother with a particular purpose. If you've lost a mother, I will give several mothers to you in North India. You too will be a mother to thousands there. Many will call you, 'Mother'! Through you, thousands will see My salvation. Through you, I will call and set apart thousands from among people speaking the language not known to you and from the land strange to you. You will have to bear many sufferings because of My name. This furnace of bitter experiences is to mould you and shape you for my purposes. I have chosen you for My ministry."

Mary surrendered herself before the voice of God, communicated to her through the prophet of God. Afterwards, she attended the meeting conducted in the church hall. In that meeting she was filled with the Holy Spirit and she began to speak to the Lord in other tongues.

When the prayer meeting concluded, the wounds and the afflictions of her heart, which she had been carrying for years, vanished. She felt a great joy, hope and divine peace in her soul.

This was a turning point in the life of Mary; since then she began to strongly grow in the Spirit giving more importance to spiritual matters than any other thing in her life.

Mary passed with good grades in her 10th grade in school. Because of her good academic achievements, there was pressure on her from people at home and the church to join a secular college for further studies; but Mary knew in her heart that God was calling her to be a missionary in North India. She decided to study in a Bible school and prepare herself to fulfil God's plan.

In those days it was not common for girls to study in a Bible School. Though words of discouragement flowed from several sources, Mary was determined in her heart not to heed to human counsel. Thus disappointing many around her, she joined the Hebron Bible School at Kumbanad.

Pastor K. E. Abraham, one of the senior leaders of the Pentecostal movement in South India, was the Principal of Hebron Bible School, Kumbanad at that time.

Mary worked hard and was a bright student in her class. When she completed her first year of studies at Hebron Bible College, Pastor K. E. Abraham and other servants of God encouraged her to continue her studies at the then Southern Asia Bible Institute (SABI), now Southern Asia Bible College (SABC), in Bangalore; they not only encouraged her to join this prestigious institution, but also, extended the needed help and support for her to join SABI.

Thus, the very next year, she enrolled for G. Th. (Graduate in Theology) program in SABI where her elder brother, P. G. Abraham, was already a student of Theology.

Mary proved her excellence in studies at SABI, by scoring the highest marks in all the subjects. She was a passionate singer too, which gave her the opportunity to be a choir member in the College. Thus she learnt numerous English hymns which are sung widely in the churches today.

Mary was greatly loved by all and she found favour among the staff too. The wife of the principal had special love and affection towards Mary, which might well have been the reason that she promised to send Mary for higher studies. Before she went home for vacation, an American woman missionary and her teacher, who always expressed a motherly love for her said, "From next year onwards, I will bear all expenses for your studies. Do not stay back for any reason whatsoever." This statement provided much solace and comfort to Mary.

As a young girl she showed unusual determination with her school work. At home she would stick to solving problems until she had completely understood them. During vacation, when she returned home, she resumed her duties and engrossed herself in the household chores and helped the family.

# 02

# A MACEDONIAN CALL

During that vacation, a magazine found its way into Mary's hands. Published from Ernakulam by Brother P. T. Xavier, it was named *Kristhuvinte Padayali* meaning 'The Soldier of Christ'.

As she was reading it, turning one page after another, an article titled *Makkadoniya Vili* translated Macedonian Call caught her attention. The article concluded with a challenge to lay down lives for the Saviour to spread the good news. As she finished reading the article, something amazing happened right there. A heavy burden and clear vision for rescuing perishing souls in North India formed inside young Mary. She hid the magazine at the bottom of her metal suitcase, lest anyone should misplace it. She secretly admired the daring spirit of the author and the message deeply touched her heart.

The article was authored by a young missionary named Thomas Mathews who was serving as a missionary in Udaipur, Rajasthan. The photo of the author was also published with the article.

Since that day Mary began to treasure the divine burden deposited within her. She started praying incessantly for the people groping in darkness, without peace and hope and without a Saviour. She committed her life to the Lord and waited on Him to fulfil His plan.

Pastor P. M. Philip, serving the Lord, at Kottayam heard about Mary and knew that she had come home for vacation. He put forth a marriage proposal for her, brought by K. V. Abraham from Udaipur. Both parties seriously considered that proposal. Finally, the prospective groom arrived in Thrissur.

The boy and his folks came to Podimannil house to see the girl. Pastor P. M. Philip, Pastor K. V. Kurien and the local minister of the Indian Pentecostal Church (IPC) at Koottala, Pastor C. V. Paul, besides the father of the boy from Punalur, were present there to advance the proposal.

According to the traditional practice, Mary brought tea for all those who had assembled there as kith and kin. Then Pastor P. M. Philip said, "Now, if Joy and Marykutty wish to talk to each other, they can."

The unexpected suggestion unnerved the boy a little; nevertheless, he asked a few questions that would soon confirm if she was going to be his future wedded wife:

"Are you willing to come to Rajasthan as a missionary?"

Mary affirmatively shook her head.

"Are you willing to come to Rajasthan soon after the marriage abandoning your studies?"

Marykutty silently stood there unable to answer that question in the presence of elders.

But Pastor P. M. Philip compelled her to answer that question.

"All will be done as my father decides...," she replied finally.

## Chapter 02

The boy had no permanent income… he had no house of his own… the church he was pastoring was a small one… worship service was being conducted in a rented building… after the marriage a series of hardships and starvation would greet her… The boy disclosed his actual condition and limitations. Then, he asked Mary:

"Are you willing to bear all these along with me?"

"Let everything be done according to the will of God," Mary replied in a low voice and slowly drew back into the kitchen.

Ultimately Marykutty's father gave his approval for the alliance and Pastor P. M. Philip stood up and announced:

"Dear all! Trusting in the Lord, the proposal for which we have assembled here is being confirmed. Next, let us schedule the date of the wedding."

Then, the two parties talked together and decided on the wedding date. It was agreed unanimously that it would take place on 9th of June, 1966.

After everyone had left, something suddenly came into Mary's memory. "Isn't the prospective groom the same person who wrote the article 'Macedonian Call' in the magazine 'The Soldier of Christ'?" she thought to herself.

As an afterthought she remembered one more thing – the prophecy she had heard through Mosha *Upadeshi!* For a minute, she closed her eyes in the presence of God and meditated. It seemed as if somebody was picking up the bits and pieces of her life and threading it into something beautiful. The realization that the marriage would be the fulfilment of God's oracle was sinking in.

But some of her relatives opposed this alliance. Anxiety cast its shadow over the Podimannil family. Finally, after a few days, Mary's father wrote a letter to the groom's father and posted it. The letter read:

"As many of my relatives have expressed their difference of opinion in marrying off our daughter, who grew up without her mother, to such a far flung place (Rajasthan), that too, as the companion of a mere twenty two year old missionary, it is difficult to hold the wedding on the 9th of June as scheduled. Hence, the marriage should be postponed to December."

The groom's folks received the letter when the wedding was close at hand. The prospective groom, Joy, along with his father went straight to Pastor P. M. Philip at Kottayam and apprised him of the situation. The father returned to Punalur but Pastor P. M. Philip and Joy decided to go and meet Mary's father. That evening on the way to Thrissur, they both attended a convention, arranged in the church of Pastor M. V. Thomas and then went to visit Mary's family in Thrissur the next evening. There was much discussion and disagreement among the two parties but finally it was decided that they would go ahead with the original scheduled date of the wedding. That night itself, both of them returned to Kottayam.

# 03

## SETTING FOOT IN UDAIPUR

Finally, 9th of June, 1966 arrived.

The bride Mary clad in a white saree was escorted to the church hall.

An audience comprising of the servants of God and relatives who came to witness the wedding packed the IPC hall at Koottala, Thrissur. Pastor Mathunny Master officiated the wedding while Pastors, V. T. Joseph and V. J. George were the main speakers. After the wedding, the relatives of the groom returned back to Punalur. Since Pastor P. M. Philip could not attend the wedding, the bride and the bridegroom alighted at Kottayam to receive blessings from Joy's mentor. They dined with him too at his residence and parted after prayer.

They then reached Hebron, Kumbanad to visit Pastor K. E. Abraham. There they ate the food prepared for them and after meeting with him, he blessed them in prayer laying his hands on them and bid them farewell. From there they went on their way to Punalur, the hometown of Joy, who is also called, Thomas Mathews.

After reaching Punalur, they stayed there for a few days. Then they came back to Thrissur and from there left for Udaipur, Rajasthan on the 30th of June.

While packing her box for the journey, Mary remembered to pack the magazine, 'The Soldier of Christ', which carried the article, 'Macedonian Call.'

A fairly large crowd of relatives and believers had assembled at the station to see off the young missionary couple. They were going to the land of Rajasthan with faith as their only possession.

The first journey of Mary to Udaipur was via Bombay (now Mumbai). Early Sunday morning, Mary and Thomas Mathews alighted from the train at Mumbai and attended the Indian Pentecostal Church (IPC) worship service conducted at Elizabeth High School, Chembur. The next morning they left from there and reached the home of Pastor Mathew Cherian in Baroda (now Vadodara) and stayed there for a day. The very next day, they set out for Udaipur.

Mary was only nineteen years old when she set her foot in Udaipur, the city of lakes, holding the hand of her twenty two-year-old husband.

Udaipur was altogether a different world for Mary! The land, the language, the culture and the attire, everything elicited surprise and interest in her.

She felt that it was a great call which had brought her to this place. She had arrived in the land of Rajputs (sons of kings) bearing a great commission. It was just the first step of a long journey. Little did she realise that challenges, hardships and difficulties also lay ahead of her. Nevertheless she knew in her heart that "God who called me is faithful. He will guide me till the end." This was the deep conviction within her heart. Mary held tightly onto the promises of God and never let them go.

## Chapter 03

Their marriage seemed to be going well during the early days when friends and acquaintances invited the newlywed couple to their homes to dine with them. The invitations and feasts ceased after a while and the new couple began to be exposed to the hardships of life.

By this time they had run out of the little amount of money which they had with them when they came from Kerala! Lack of money was to become a constant companion for this new family.

A period of emptiness and starvation was setting in.

It was a new beginning and there were only a handful of believers in the church. The couple did not let them know about their lack of money and unmet personal needs. All of them thought that the new couple would have saved enough money!

In spite of the different struggles they encountered, Thomas and Mary braved the storms of life together and never allowed the waves to drown them. They moved through the length and breadth of the city sharing the good news, speaking, showing acts of kindness and helping anyone in need, showing the grace and mercy of our Lord.

Those days Thomas rode the bicycle and Mary often accompanied him by sitting on the back of the bicycle. They visited the homes of the believers, encouraged and prayed for them. Though they would have tea and snacks from those homes, they declined to have meals unless they were invited beforehand.

Most days they had food only once on a given day. Often, tea and bun was their only food for the day.

Sometimes there was no food at all for them to eat and Thomas would feel ashamed to look at the face of his new wife. It was a painful experience they underwent.

But on such occasions, Mary displayed her deep belief in God's abiding will and did not grumble even once or say words that would dent the confidence and courage of her husband. Rather than looking at the situation, she would look towards the face of God and boost the morale of her husband in every way possible.

Some monetary support that trickled in from different places was spent for the expansion of the Lord's work and nothing was left to supply the domestic needs.

Although the church in the city and its activities were expanding through signs, wonders and various miracles, the church was not yet self-sufficient to meet the needs of the pastor and his family. Besides, as activities increased, more money was required for the church expansion. Even though the expenses were on the rise, there was no increase in the income at all.

On one hand, evangelism was expanding and on the other starvation and hardships multiplied.

# 04

---

# NOT BY SIGHT BUT BY FAITH

One day a servant of God came from a distant place. Only Mary was at home then. The time was nearing noon and she had to serve food to the servant of God who arrived tired after the day's long journey. But, even the rice needed to cook a small meal of rice gruel was not there at home. Nor were there any other provisions in the kitchen to feed the servant of God. Mary was worried as she had no idea what to do.

Usually, in such circumstances, she used to sell old newspapers and meet the need at hand. As usual, she went and collected the newspapers, but the papers could not add up even to a mere kilogram. They had already sold all the old newspapers few weeks before, when such a similar need had arisen.

However, she had to serve food to the visitor. She took whatever newspapers were lying there and came to the road through the back door and approached the shop from where they used to buy provisions. The shopkeeper weighed the newspapers and asked her why she had come with only a few newspapers. Mary was perplexed as she did not know what to say. Nevertheless, she managed to reply without looking at his face: "I need some rice." Without saying anything further, the shopkeeper weighed half a kilogram of rice and gave it to her.

She quickly reached home and began to cook the rice. But before the rice could be cooked the stove ran out of fuel and the fire died. When she checked she found there was no kerosene left in the stove! A bottle of kerosene cost only four annas (quarter of rupee) then, but she did not even have that in her hand. However, she tried to work on the stove; thanking and praising God, she began pumping the stove. What a miracle! The stove which had no kerosene in it burnt bright and the rice began to boil. After a while, the stove went out again. Mary was not willing to accept defeat; she repeatedly pumped the stove with faith and it burnt again. As soon as the rice was cooked, the stove stopped burning. She served the visitor the rice that had been cooked with a little pickle. That servant of God ate the food and left happily after praying for the missionary family.

Though, those were the days of spiritual progress, the year 1966 passed through with much physical hardship and tears for the young Mathews family.

Most of the time, Pastor Mathews would be on long trips in connection with the work of the Lord. While leaving home, he would take with him whatever meagre amount of money they had to meet the travelling expenses. There would be nothing left to give for domestic expenses. On such occasions, Mary would encourage her husband by saying: "Don't you worry thinking about household supplies. Do the Lord's work wherever He sends you. God will provide for me."

One day Mary's elder brother Pastor Abraham turned up in Udaipur. They did not quite expect him as they received the letter he had sent to intimate them of his visit, only that morning. A year had passed by after Mary's marriage and Pastor Abraham came with the intention of enquiring about the wellbeing of his sister and brother-in-law and also to visit the areas of their work. On this occasion too, Mary was alone at home.

Thomas had gone to a distant village for the Lord's work. The condition which prevailed at home was of abject poverty; Mary was not in a position to make even a cup of tea for her brother as there was not even a pinch of tea powder or sugar left in the kitchen.

After marriage, this was the first time when someone from her family was visiting Mary. She was sad and worried that she could not treat her brother well. Unable to bear the grief, she wept before God for a while. With tears welling up her eyes, she sat at the steps of the backyard looking out aimlessly.

Her brother had arrived very tired after a long train journey of three days. She knew she had to serve her brother some tea or coffee to drink and also food to eat. There seemed to be no solution. Her tears rolled down her cheeks and fell on the ground as she sat on the steps in the backyard. Suddenly she saw something glittering in the soil. She kicked the soil with her feet to see what it was. She could not believe her eyes. It was a one rupee silver coin! When she picked it up, she saw another four coins lying around – five rupees in total! She ran to the second storey of the building and asked the people sitting there whether it belonged to them. They all replied in the negative. Praising God she went to the nearby shop, bought provisions to make coffee and food and returned home before her brother finished bathing.

She praised God with a thankful heart for this divine provision.

Numerous other stories of God's miraculous provision abounded. On one occasion, Mary's father reached Udaipur desiring to see his daughter and her family who were engaged in Gospel work in the faraway land, Rajasthan. Again, though he had sent a letter to intimate them of his visit, it did not reach them on time. When he reached their house after locating it by the address he had with him, the sun was about to set. Giving food to the father who had arrived exhausted from the long journey was then wishful thinking for Mary. Pastor Mathews was away from home on one of his usual missionary trips. Mary was perplexed and did not know what to do.

Neither did the daughter say anything about dinner, nor did the father ask anything. Due to excessive fatigue, he had drifted off to sleep.

When he woke up in the morning, Mary made a cup of black coffee for him. She was in tremendous agony as she had not served any dinner to her father and there was no provision for breakfast too. With much grief, she went to the backyard of the house and sat there. It was then that a brother named Philip Thayyil reached there. Philip was a friend of Pastor and used to visit them often. When he saw Mary sitting with eyes reddened because of her tears, he went straight to the kitchen. He saw only the kettle in which the coffee was made; there were no signs of breakfast preparation. All the containers were empty.

Philip Thayyil went outside with a bag. He returned after buying all the necessary provisions like rice, vegetables and eggs from a shop in the locality. Without saying a word he left the bag in the kitchen and went his way.

Though, Mary saw the provisions which reached her kitchen, she was unable to react for a while. Thus Mary experienced the miraculous provisions of God and saw her needs being met in a divine manner through angels and through people, time and again.

# 05

---

# HAND OF GOD REVEALED IN THE LAST HOUR

A long period of starvation and poverty followed this young couple. Unable to lead a respectable life in the society, one day because of the impoverished lifestyle, Mary shared a thought with her husband:

"Both of us are young and healthy; hence, we may be able to endure many more bouts of hunger and persistent poverty. But just imagine what will happen if a child is born to us in this situation. So, it is better not to have a child now. I cannot bear the sight of our children starving with us. We should not have children now. Why should we drag them into such hardship?"

The words of his dear wife rattled Mathews. Mary had said such words due to the constant state of hunger and deprivation they faced.

Mathews replied, "Let us commit this matter into the hands of God. I believe God will provide for the needs of our children. However, if God wills that we should not have children, so be it. Even if we don't have children biologically born to us, God will give us spiritual children. After all, why should we worry about our children who are not yet born? Let everything happen according to the will of God!"

Finally, the will of God prevailed. Mary became pregnant!

On the evening of 30th April, 1968, Mary began having labour pains. At that time, other than her husband, nobody was near her. Eight annas (half a rupee) was all what was needed to take her to the hospital in a horse cart. But they did not have even that paltry sum of money. Finally, leaning on her husband, Mary somehow reached the hospital. Pastor Mathews was praying as he paced up and down the corridor, outside the labour room. By the grace of God, Mary delivered normally and gave birth to a female child on May 1st, 1968. She was called Grace. When the morning dawned, a nurse called out to Pastor Mathews and said, "Go and quickly bring powder to put on the child's body, a towel to wrap the child and two small frocks. You should have brought these beforehand!"

The previous night Mary had walked to the hospital in labour pain because they lacked the meagre sum to hire a horse cart. Now Mathews wondered how he could buy powder and frocks for his newborn baby?

With unbearable sorrow, but, hoping against hope, that somehow a way would open up, Pastor Mathews wandered outside the hospital and near the post office. No way seemed to open up before him. No money order came from anywhere. All this while, Mary was lying beside the new-born baby without anyone near her to help her. While walking back to the hospital empty handed, Mathews secretly prayed, "Lord, that nurse should not be there!" But he ended up right in front of her. As soon as she saw him, she cast aspersions on him in front of others and her words struck him like arrows. "Are you a man? How come you are so irresponsible?" Having lost words, he heard all that she said with his head bowed. Gradually, God started to work through several people who came and helped. All arrangements were done for the wellbeing of the mother and child and they were discharged after spending six days in the hospital.

Days passed by. They could not give enough milk and food to the baby and because of that she continuously fell ill.

Although they had decided that they would not borrow anything from anybody, when hunger became unbearable, one kilogram of rice was borrowed from a nearby provision store. They used the rice bought on the morning of 21st sparingly and they survived with it till the 24th. They spoon-fed the baby *kanji vellam* (water from rice porridge) in the place of milk. Finally when there was no more rice, the baby's *kanji vellam* also stopped. On 24th they received a money order for a hundred and fifty rupees. A message was written in the money order coupon which said: "I had lost four-hundred rupees some time back. On getting that back, an amount of one hundred and fifty rupees is being sent for the Lord's work."

After some time, a brother asked Thomas and Mary if they could receive a Canadian woman missionary, Elva Clapp, who was due to arrive in Udaipur. When she arrived at the railway station, Mathews carried her large box and bedroll on his head for some distance up to the horse cart as they failed to get a coolie. This act by a respectable evangelist greatly touched that lady. The next day when she departed, she handed over one hundred and fifteen rupees to Mary.

The money thus received from various sources was spent for the house rent, the needs of fellow brethren, missionary journeys and to meet the needs of others. Financial trouble came to haunt them again sooner than expected and the family drifted towards starvation. They were on the edge of starvation, when a brother named David Raj brought 10 kg wheat for them. As he had no money to help them, he had borrowed the wheat from the store of the company he worked for. Thus, God miraculously delivered the Mathews' from hunger and deprivation at several occasions, through several people, in times of dire need.

At another time, they were in trouble again, going without food. The family had been starving thus for about a week. Then, a brother named

Vakthabhai, came on foot from a village Pai, a place about 30 kilometres from Udaipur, carrying 15 kg of wheat and 1 kg ghee (butter) and handed over the provisions to Mary. The flour had been kept in his home to make food for his family, and the ghee had been kept to be sold. On being prompted by the spirit of God while sitting at home, he walked all that distance to bring them the provisions. It was after many days that they could taste chapattis cooked with ghee.

On another occasion, Udaipur was under a severe heat wave and they did not have a single fan at home. The baby kept crying unable to bear the excessive heat. The sight of the baby crying incessantly was too much for a Jacobite friend named Baby. He went to a nearby shop selling fans, and brought a green coloured table fan, manufactured by the Usha company after paying the first instalment of ten rupees and standing as the guarantor for the rest of the instalments. Thus, Mathews got a fan in 1968 after withstanding five years of excessive heat. They used the fan in the prayer hall during prayer meetings and inside the room, the rest of the time. Whenever it was difficult to pay an instalment, the dear brother C. Baby helped them by paying it. He retired as an Executive Engineer after a long career in government service in Udaipur.

# 06

# AMAZING GRACE

Grace, the oldest daughter of Thomas and Mary, was literally born into depravation and did not receive proper food or clothes. She was breast fed only for three months in her infancy as the mother lacked proper nutrition. After that, her parents could not buy milk for her everyday; they gave her black tea instead. The thought that they could not even provide enough milk for the child caused them much anguish. One of those days, a brother from Kuwait named George Mathew sent seven big tins of full cream milk powder of the Nestle brand for the child. Though, it would have been more than sufficient for her for a fairly long period, her parents also used it to satiate their hunger by consuming it, mixing it with water. As the milk powder profited the whole starving family, the stock did not last long.

It was the last week of December, 1969. The Christmas season had arrived. Most Christian homes wore a festive look. When Christmas cake and other delicacies brought cheers and celebrations to the children in those homes, Mary's home was devoid of all these. Suddenly, she heard someone knocking at the door. Mary opened the door and saw an unknown woman greeting her. She introduced herself and said, "I am Mrs. Rudra working in the Bible Society as Promotional Secretary. I have come to Udaipur for some urgent work. I came via Jaipur and yesterday when I left from there, Dr. Mrs. Peters gave me this to hand over to you." Saying this, the visitor gave Mary a basket full of various fruits. When she opened it, she was astonished; sweet lemon, sapodilla, apple, orange and other fruits weighing more than ten kilograms filled the basket! The subsequent four to five days, they ate just fruits for food.

Waking up one morning, Grace oddly began to cry, asking for an apple. All attempts to pacify her were to no avail. It was not usual for the family to buy apples. There was no money left to buy an apple for the child who kept crying for it. After a while, Mary was cleaning the room where they put up guests who visited them. Cleaning beneath the bed, she felt something striking against the broom and she stooped to see. There, beneath the bed, lay two apples! The previous night a family from Zawar Mines had stayed with them as guests. She guessed that the apples might have dropped from their bag unknowingly when they left in the morning, after sleeping in that room. She soon went to the child who was crying unceasingly to get an apple and gave two apples to her in place of one. Then, she praised and thanked God, who hears the cries and provides for His saints.

Once when Grace was studying in a convent school, they could not pay her fees due to financial constraints. Two months' fees had to be paid. One day, during the morning assembly, the mother who was in charge of the school humiliated Grace mentioning about the non-payment of fees in front of other children. After the assembly, the mother restrained her from entering the classroom and made her stand in the sun for a long time. Finally, she was sent back home.

Grace was crying as she walked towards her house all alone. With tears rolling down her cheeks, she narrated to her parents the events that had happened at the school. Though they understood the gravity of the overt insult suffered by their child, they did not have any means to pay the fees any time sooner. It was only after a few days, when some money came along, that they could pay the fees. The reasons for the delay in the payment were explained to the school management and Grace resumed attending school.

Grace did not have too many clothes to change and wear. She only had two sets of skirts and blouses which she wore to the school for three years. Due to constant wash, they had lost their shine and had become threadbare. One of her dresses was torn a little. One day she went to school wearing the torn dress. She covered the rip holding her school bag against it.

As Grace was walking to the classroom, her teacher was watching her standing in the corridor. The teacher grabbed her by the threadbare skirt she was wearing and asked angrily, "Is this the kind of dress you wear to school? Do not come in such a dress in future." It was a stern warning.

Meanwhile, the part of the skirt the teacher had pulled tore downwards. It was unintentional, but the skirt was so old that it ripped apart when she grabbed the child. Grace felt very sad and helpless. She took a safety pin from her friend and fastened it to the skirt to hold the torn parts together. Ashamed to appear before other students wearing the torn skirt, Grace returned home crying.

A sister in the church who came to know about the matter, secretly gave Mary a skirt and blouse which belonged to her daughter, a student of the same school. The next day, Grace went to the school wearing that pair which looked comparatively new.

Grace studied in a school where the students were from affluent families. All her friends came to school displaying the affluence of their homes. They often expressed the desire to visit her home, but, she spurned them. Because, if they came visiting, there were no chairs for them to sit in also, there was no good food to be given to them. Even when friends invited her to birthday celebrations and other such events, she consciously avoided attending them because when her friends would come wearing expensive dresses, she had to turn up in her ragged school uniform, the only clothes she had to wear outside.

Grace often went to school without having proper food. Almost every morning when she left for school, Mary would tell her, "I will bring your lunch to the school later."

During lunch time, Grace would stand at the gate expectantly. But, more often than not, she would be waiting in vain. Her mum would not turn up. How could Mary bring any food for her daughter when there was nothing at home?

There was an *ayah* (a person who helps smaller children) named Ruth in that school. One day, she happened to notice Grace. When other students sat in a circle and joyously ate their lunch, Grace stood at the gate alone and waited for someone and returned dejected. The *ayah* soon took Grace along with her and gave a share of her lunch to the child.

On the following days too, the *ayah* saw Grace waiting at the gate in vain and return to the class. Often, she would share her meal with the child. As Grace used to come to school without having breakfast, she ate her portion ravenously.

Rarely did Grace bring lunch to school. On one such rare occasion when she had indeed brought lunch, it was not proper food. One day, as a side dish for chapatti, it was dry coconut chutney powder, which someone had brought from Kerala.

Children who were having their sumptuous lunch regarded her with contempt when they saw her eating the chapattis with dry coconut chutney powder and laughed at her. She became very upset. Thereafter, she did not have lunch along with her classmates even once. Hence, on a positive note, they did not come to know that she did not have lunch on most days.

Among all their children, the eldest daughter Grace endured the most hardships. However, she excelled in academics. She was chosen the best student of the school when she completed her high school education. Everyone praised her.

# 07

# GOD'S GLORY AND PROVISION IN THE DESERT

Times of hardships extended beyond anyone's comprehension. With ferocity, the rains of adversities lashed against Mary and her family.

To share this life of hunger and deprivations, a new member joined the family.

On 16th July, 1971, Mary gave birth to their second daughter. The parents named her Glory. The name implied their desire that the glory of God would be revealed through her in the days to come. They dedicated her to the Lord's work with prayer.

Like Grace, Glory too grew up amidst poverty and hardships. She did not have good food to eat and decent clothes to wear; hence, she followed the example set by her parents and practically learnt the lessons of a life of faith.

Grace and Glory both went to a school where the children from the rich families in Udaipur studied. Though there was no source of income, their parents saw to it that they studied in the best school of the city. Perhaps, they were the poorest students of the school.

They lacked proper food and good clothes; often, they did not take lunch to the school. During lunchtime, when other children ate their lunch, Grace and Glory went away and sat in the shade of a tree. On most days, Mary could not bring lunch for them. Then, Grace and Glory would walk straightaway to the water tap and drink enough water to fill their stomachs as a means of satiating their hunger. After that, they would sit under the shade of a tree until the bell rang again.

Meanwhile, a parcel from America reached their home unexpectedly. The family was curious to find out who had sent this parcel for them. When they saw the address of the sender, it was Alice Chevenek. Earlier, during her visit to India, Alice had made an acquaintance with Pastor Mathews. They opened the parcel with eagerness; they could not believe their eyes when they saw the contents – beautiful clothes for Grace and Glory! The clothes looked expensive, even more expensive than what most of their classmates wore.

As she took the clothes in her hands, Mary's eyes welled up with tears of joy and thankfulness to God.

As Grace and Glory further experienced God's mercy and provision, their faith and dependence on the Lord kept on increasing.

On one occasion, brother George Mathew came to Kerala from Kuwait and asked Pastor Mathews to reach there immediately. He also sent the money needed for travelling along with his letter. When Pastor Mathews was returning from Kerala, the brother gave him a suitcase filled with clothes. It contained a saree for Mary, frocks for the children and foreign fabric for the Pastor to get a suit made. It was indeed a miraculous provision.

The miracle of provision was always mixed with the miracle of sacrificial giving in the home of Pastor Thomas and Mary Mathews.

## Chapter 07

Once when Pastor Mathews and Mary returned after visiting the United States of America, Glory was harbouring great expectations. As she did not have good clothes to wear like the girls of her age, naturally she expected her parents to bring good frocks from the US. But contrary to her expectations, they did not bring frocks and other clothes for the children. Glory became very upset and asked her mummy why they did not bring any frock. The reply she got was: "Daughter, shops in America don't sell frocks." Glory believed her mother's words then. Only many years later did she understand that her parents collected whatever money they had received and spent it for supporting co-workers and for various needs arising in the Lord's work without even buying clothes for their own children.

Another picture Glory has in mind of her mother is that of her bringing as many books as she could collect on foreign tours, without bringing anything else! As funds were not sufficient for buying books for the Bible college library, wherever she went she used to collect the books others gave her and carried it alone. Once, as a result of bringing such a heavy load of books, her hand had swollen. But Mary would not give up.

Many years later, one Christmas day, the nuns and other teachers from the school, where Grace studied, came to her home in a van. They said to them, "We had never known that you were working here without a salary. Had we known this, we would have never taken a tough stand on the remittance of the fees of your children. We regret that."

The nuns gifted the children sweets, cake, clothes, shoes and other things saying, "These are our Christmas gifts for you!"

# 08

# MANOHAR BHAWAN AT CHETAK CIRCLE

At the heart of Udaipur city, near Chetak Circle, a building belonging to the royal family of Bedla was situated. The name of the building was Manohar Bhawan.

It was to Manohar Bhawan, 110 Chetak Marg, that Pastor Mathews had brought Mary after their wedding. Hence, Mary had a special emotional connection with the building. She had experienced numerous vicissitudes of life, ups and downs, and sorrows and joys there. The house had witnessed countless wonderful acts of God too.

But then, a crisis surfaced. The owner of the building, Rao Manohar Singh, who had loved them very much during the earlier ·days and let out the house to them at a cheap rent, had sold the building to one Mehta, a rich businessman. The new owner wanting to evict the tenants, sent a legal notice asking them to move out within thirty days i.e. before the 15th of August. Pastor Mathews began searching for a new house to move into within the stipulated time.

As for Mary, it was agonizing even to think of moving out of Manohar Bhawan. They had been staying in that house consisting of nine rooms, paying only a meagre amount as rent. All her three children were born and brought up in that house. Manohar Bhawan was a convenient place for all things – the schooling of the children, worship service, Bible school, printing press, etc. It was difficult to get a house like that there; and even if they got one, they would have to pay a heavy monthly rent which would be impossible in the financial problems they faced. Overwhelmed by those thoughts, Mary prayed to God with tears to bring them out of this crisis.

Within the allowed time period itself, they rented a two-room house at Bhupalpura, a corner of the city, and shifted household goods there. But, they kept a bed and some sundry items in Manohar Bhawan itself thinking that they could use them till 15th. On the night of 14th they conducted what would have been the last prayer meeting at Manohar Bhawan. As the children of God were standing and praising God, a scripture portion emerged clear to Pastor Mathews: "But you will not leave in haste or go in flight; for the LORD will go before you, the God of Israel will be your rear guard" (Isaiah 52: 12). He read out the verse aloud and asked the gathering to thank God for this promise. When he said, "God is going to work a miracle; let us receive it tonight by faith," all of them praised and glorified God in a loud voice.

That night, believers stayed there for long and departed for their homes late, after the meeting was over. As they were leaving late in the night, Pastor Mathews said, "As the rest of the goods need to be shifted, the believers who live nearby should come and help me move in the morning, before going to work."

That night something strange happened. The time was around 11.30 in the night and it was raining heavily. Somebody was knocking on the door loudly. When they strained their ears and listened, they heard someone shouting, "Pastor *sahib,* please, come outside!" They doubted whether Mehta's men had come to harm or forcefully evict them thinking that they would not move out. Anxiety nagged their minds. Fearing there was something wrong in the air, Mary warned Pastor Mathews not to open the door, but he went and opened the door. To their surprise, they found Mr Mehta and his wife, the new owners of the building, standing outside while it was still heavily pouring.

"Please, come inside! Why are you standing outside?" Pastor said wondering what brought them there at that time of the night.

"I am drunk; so, I will not come inside the house where you conduct worship meetings. Besides, you may not believe what I am going to say. That is why I brought my wife along with me." Then Mehta looked at his wife and told her, "You must explain things to Pastor *sahib.*"

She said, "As usual, after taking drinks my husband went to bed at 10.30 p.m. After some time, he felt severe pain in the chest. Despite taking medicines, there was no respite at all. Then he got up and began to perform *pooja* (Hindu worship rites). As he was doing this, *Bhagwan* (God) told him, 'You just go and tell the *padri* (Pastor) not to vacate the house. Tell him he can buy the house too.' Therefore, you don't have to come with the key of the house tomorrow. We have also decided that you can purchase the building and give the money to us in instalments."

As soon as she stopped speaking, they went to their car and got into it. Unable to believe what he heard, Pastor Mathews ran towards the car asking, "One minute, sir! Which *Bhagwan* told you this?"

Mr. Mehta replied, "Your *Yeshu Bhagwan* himself. Which other *Bhagwan* will speak like that? You just go and sleep, don't come to me with the key tomorrow..."

Pastor went back inside the house. Bewildered, he shared what he heard with his wife Mary. That night both of them thanked the living God. Try as they might, they were not able to sleep. They lay on the bed silently meditating on this awesome God. They woke up early in the morning and passed the news to the members of the church. That day itself, he visited Mehta at his home and thanked him for his generosity;

he consented to buy the building for sixty thousand rupees. He came back after promising by faith that he would make the payment by the end of December that year.

This development was a sweet reply from God to the tearful prayers of Mary.

This event took place in the year 1978 and Pastor Mathews wrote about it in *'Cross & Crown'* magazine. On reading about the willingness of the owner to sell the building and the need of sixty thousand rupees to buy it, Brother Philip Thayyil, who had now moved to the middle East, got excited and invited Pastor Mathews to visit Muscat.

The visa and the other needed documents and some money for the travel arrived from Muscat. The trip was a blessing in many ways. God opened many financial sources and they were able to buy the building before the end of the year, as promised earlier.

Along with that, God gave another blessing. There was enough money to buy a new scooter too. This was their first scooter in sixteen years. For sixteen years, they had traversed the roads on bicycle. Now Pastor Mathews and Mary were able to ride the scooter, praising and thanking God.

**09**

# AN INHERITANCE AMONG THE NATIVES

It was not on the soil of North India, but rather, in the hearts of the people there that Mary found a place for herself. The best example of her close knit ties with them can be located in a village called Pai, thirty kilometres from Udaipur.

Many years ago, in the village of Pai, there was a chieftain who was both a robber and hunter. He had no qualms about stealing or robbing. Both the public as well as the police were fed up with him. One day Jesus came into the life of a man named Vakthabhai. He became a new creation in all areas of his life. It was this Vakthabhai who brought 15 kg wheat and some ghee on foot from a distance of thirty kilometres, carrying the whole weight on his head to feed Mary and family when they had been starving.

For Vakthabhai, Mary was a daughter not born to him. He used to call her 'the daughter in Udaipur.' That expression of affection was not mere rhetoric. Before departing from this world he instructed his children thus: "Whenever you divide our land, give one share of it to my daughter in Udaipur."

Though, Vakthabhai went to be with the Lord, his children absolutely obeyed their father's instruction. When the land was measured and divided, they set apart an equal portion for 'the daughter in Udaipur' as they had done for themselves, his biological children. But, Mary refused to take the whole share of land they gave her. From the portion allotted to her, she accepted only as much as needed for building a church hall. Today, a beautiful church building stands on that piece of land.

According to His promises, God not only gave several mothers to Mary, he also gave her many fathers like Vakthabhai!

# 10

# HE WILL COMMAND HIS ANGELS

Mary often went on missionary journeys on such unsafe paths which even men feared to tread. On many journeys she was alone without co-workers, team members or assistants. That she emerged unhurt without a scratch or bruise from those lonely journeys she had been undertaking for a fairly long period demonstrates the constant protection and watch provided by the angels of God. Two incidents narrated below underscore the veracity of this inference.

Once, Mary was riding her scooter alone from Udaipur city to the Filadelfia campus near Sanjay Park. Those days, there were no streetlights like the ones shining today; the roads were empty and stark darkness prevailed everywhere. Mary did not usually become unsettled or frightened that easily. But, that day when she reached a certain place, all of a sudden, fear gripped her. Mary clearly sensed at once that someone had soon taken over the control of the scooter. Then all the way to the campus, that invisible force controlled the scooter. Mary just sat there learning a new lesson. She felt, as if an angel of the Lord had driven the scooter for her that night.

A similar incident took place in 1972. The wedding of a sister who was a member of the Udaipur church was to be solemnized at Kottayam. Mary had reached Kottayam to attend the wedding. After the wedding, she went to Punalur to visit her husband's relatives. When she reached there, it was night. The path looked desolate and it was pitch dark outside. Fear crept into her mind. It was past 9.30 pm. She walked along the railway track praying. Suddenly, in the dim moonlight, she saw the sight of two turbaned men walking in front of her. Mary felt a huge relief. She walked with brisk steps to catch up with them.

The thought that they were going on the same path she had to go, completely dispelled her fear. After walking for a while, she reached her husband's home. But, the men who walked in front of her disappeared at once! Her mother-in-law, who had been waiting for her, came outside the house. When she told her about the two men who walked in front of her, the elderly woman said without hesitation that no one in that place fits the description.

Certainly, they might have been the angels of God!

Mary did not remain a mere shadow of her brilliant and renowned husband. The assessment that Mary surged ahead in the Lord's work matching the steps of a husband like Dr. Thomas Mathews, a man with an exceptional personality and one of the most powerful Christian leaders in North India, should make us understand how profound the grace of God that worked in her was and how deep her commitment was!

Once, Pastor Mathews remarked about his wife thus:

"When we reach heaven and receive the reward for winning souls, I believe that my wife will get sixty percent of it and I will get only forty percent. She has suffered more than me."

## Chapter 10

Dr. Thomas Mathews used to give an allegory to explain the difference between him and his wife which became very famous later on. He used to say:

"I am the 'accelerator' and my wife is the 'brake.'"

The witty allegory implied that many of his somewhat impractical and unwise decisions hurriedly taken without thinking of the consequences could be reconsidered and corrected by the timely and gentle interventions of his sensible wife. Mary had been to Pastor Mathews, a Proverbs 31 wife.

# 11

---

# MIRACLES OF HEALING
# WROUGHT THROUGH PRAYERS

It was 1974. Mary was pregnant with her third child. By July, she had completed her fifth month of pregnancy. One day she began to feel unbearable pain in her stomach while a prayer meeting was in progress at the Gospel Centre, formerly called Manohar Bhawan. Despite her strong wish, she was unable to attend the meeting due to unbearable pain. As the pain swept through her body she lost all her strength. She went to the steps at the backyard and lay down after spreading something on the floor.

She lay there thinking that the pain would go away. But the pain persisted. With the passing of each day the pain only intensified. She was finally taken to the doctor for a check-up. When the doctor examined her, she was diagnosed with appendicitis, a condition characterized by inflammation of the appendix, and she was already in a critical stage. The doctor advised immediate surgery (appendectomy) to remove the vermiform appendix. Apprehension gripped everyone because of the risk of danger involved in surgery during pregnancy. Administering anaesthesia to a pregnant woman might endanger the life of the child in the womb. The antibiotics and other medicines prescribed for the expectant mother after surgery might also affect the foetus in various ways. But it was impossible to evade the surgery as infection had lethally spread near the fallopian tube and was threatening to benumb the organs by blocking the blood circulation there.

The surgeon at the Udaipur Medical College disclosed a shocking truth before the surgery as he was left with no other option, "This is a very risky operation. Now, no guarantee whatsoever can be given. The life of either the mother or the child is in danger."

Though the warning of the doctor was frightening, there was no other solution left. The surgery was inevitable as the infection had been rapidly spreading with each passing day.

Mary was sent to the operation theatre with prayers.

Staff nurses who used to attend the worship service at the Gospel Centre, including one sister Susan, who is now in New York city, were on duty inside the operation theatre.

Moments of anxiety and fear crept up. Who would survive the surgery – the mother or the child? As nobody had the answer, everyone kept praying to God, the ultimate source of answer or solution to any question or problem.

After the surgery, Sister Susan showed Mary the removed part of the appendix which resembled more or less, a bunch of grapes.

The surgery was a success. God did not allow any disaster to happen to either of them. God safeguarded the lives of the mother and the child in her womb.

On 13th November, 1974, Mary delivered the child who would have died without seeing the light of day. After the birth of two girls, a boy was born to them!

## Chapter 11

Pappa, Mummy, Grace and Glory affectionately called him Babu. When Babu grew up, he came to be known as Paul Mathews.

In 1982, arthritis severely affected Mary and her condition deteriorated. She suffered intense pain and allied complications. Ultimately, as she could not stretch both her legs and became unable to even perform the morning routines, her life turned miserable. A bed was there which belonged to Mrs. D. P. Roy, the former District Education Officer of Udaipur. Mary lay on it trying to suppress the unbearable pain. Many days had passed and Mary could not stretch her legs.

One night, she felt unbearable pain crushing her. She almost cried aloud in pain. Hearing his mother's cry, Babu, who was sleeping beside her woke up suddenly. He became very upset seeing the condition of his mother who was writhing in severe pain. The boy who was just eight years old then, prayed for the healing of his mother in the manner he knew best. And a miracle ensued! Mary felt the pain recede in her legs and gradually, she experienced much relief. With the pain having decreased considerably, the mother slowly fell into sound sleep. The son had already fallen asleep by then.

During that deep sleep, Mary happened to see a vision coming alive. A multitude of hands were touching her arthritis stricken legs!

When Mary woke up after a pleasant sleep, she felt energetic! She was overcome by surprise, she had been unable to stand or walk properly for days on end; but, it seemed that not even a single sign of arthritis remained in her body, she was experiencing total relief.

Suddenly, she remembered the previous night's vision in which she had seen the hands of many people placed on her legs. She realized that God was revealing to her through the vision that unknown to her, several people had been praying for her. After these two incidents, arthritis never again nagged her in life. Not only that, the next week itself, she was able to travel to Ahwa situated in the Dang district of Gujarat for participating in Gospel activities. When she reached there, a big crisis awaited her. A *hartal,* meaning total shutdown of government institutions, shops and traffic had been announced in that region and no vehicle was plying! There was no way that she could reach the destination. But because of the healing that she received, Mary covered a distance of several kilometers on foot that day with a sister named Honi, called Honey by Mary.

In a situation where she could not set her feet on the ground due to severe arthritic pain, this change had happened when God touched her in two phases, first through her eight year old son, Babu, alias Paul, and then through a vision of multitudes of people laying hands on her.

# 12

# LIGHT IN THE DARKNESS

The name Kotra used to elicit fear among people. This village in the interior of Rajasthan used to be the place where people were sent when they were to be punished severely. No one wanted to go there, not even to visit. It was indeed a dark place, spiritually and physically.

It was in the year 1980 that Pastor Mathews heard about a missionary who served the poor and sick in Kotra many decades ago. Missionary stories had often challenged Pastor Mathews to launch out further. Being inquisitive, he travelled to Kotra to view the land and to see the people.

On reaching this village which was cut off from normal civilization, he was deeply moved to see the plight of people. They were totally illiterate, had poor living conditions and were moving about with bows and arrows in their hands. This sight broke Pastor Mathews' heart. On reaching there, he also heard that this place was called the place of black waters, meaning a tough place. People working in the government offices, were transferred and posted there when they were being punished!

He returned from the place with a burden to reach out and help these people. He shared his heart with Mary. A few days later, he returned to Kotra with a bundle of tracts and gospel literature along with an evangelist, Brother David Masih. They left Udaipur with a burning passion to reach out to these people but things did not turn out to be all that favourable.

As they were distributing gospel tracts standing on the muddy roads, and sharing about the love of Jesus to the people, some people strongly opposed them and chased them away. There was no other option left for them but to return home. Several other attempts were also made to return to the land with the gospel bundles but it seemed to be futile because the people were totally hostile.

One day while he was visiting Kotra again, he met his classmate and friend, a Muslim young man, who asked him to start a school for the neglected people. This seemed to be the best way to continue to work in the area. Pastor Mathews realized it was important to meet the needs of the people and also to have access to them.

He decided to start a children's home along with the school. After a few days he returned to Kotra with Mary and took five children with him under his care in a rented a building. Few of the Bible College students were assigned to take care and teach these children. For a year, this is how the ministry continued in Kotra.

In the year 1982, when Pastor Mathews and his family were on a rare get together with their extended family, on the joyous occasion of Mary's brother's wedding, they suddenly received a not-so-happy telegram from home. It read something like this, "All our things have been thrown out and we are in jail. Please come immediately." This telegram was from the brothers who had been placed in Kotra at that time.

## Chapter 12

What could be done? At such crucial junctures, it always fell on Mary to come up with a solution. She committed to go back to Udaipur right after the wedding and then to Kotra. The wedding festivities being over, she boarded the train to take the three day journey back to Udaipur and then on to Kotra. When she reached there, God had prepared people to help her to talk to the police and also help bring the men out of the prison. It was a great miracle indeed.

When the people refused to give them a room to further run the school, she hired the corridor of the house of a rich man there and began to run the school. It was tough, but once Mary had made up her mind, there was no going back. She stayed there for weeks and months to ensure that all things were being properly done.

With only one bus plying between Kotra and Udaipur in those days, travelling was the toughest part. The hundred and twenty kilometer journey used to take anywhere between four to five hours. But that did not stop Mary.

On one occasion, while returning from Kotra, her bus broke down halfway. There was nothing that could be done. Either they had to wait there the whole day or go back to Kotra. She and some other co-passengers decided to walk back to Udaipur. With her luggage and other school supplies, she walked back for over 60 kms to Udaipur in the pouring rain!

Today the ministry in and around Kotra stands as a testimony of what God can do, when we are totally committed to Him.

Children who had no opportunity to study were taken under care and taught to read and write. Many of them are now government employees while others have taken on other professions.

In adverse conditions too, Mary accepted her God – ordained role not only in the family or church but also in the community. She devoted her life to the development of children, women and families as well.

Mary's contribution to the mission work that started in Udaipur is invaluable.

# 13

# EVOLUTION OF A WOMAN MISSIONARY

It was mentioned earlier in this book that the marriage proposal to marry Pastor Mathews came up unexpectedly when Mary had arrived on her first vacation to Kerala from Southern Asia Bible Institute, where she was studying for her G. Th. program and shortly after the wedding, she accompanied him to Udaipur.

Mary felt considerably disappointed when her marriage put a pause to her ambition of completing her theological education.

Although Mary had not said anything about it to Pastor Mathews, he read the mind of his beloved wife, and took the initiative to help her achieve her dream. He gave her all the encouragement she needed and made the necessary arrangements for her to complete her B. Th. from Allahabad Bible Seminary and B. D. from Serampore

University. Today she is a competent teacher at the Filadelfia Bible College, Udaipur, besides being a popular speaker on the North Indian convention stages.

It was during the Diwali vacation of 1966 that Mary first went to the villages for evangelistic activities.

The first village she visited was Bagpura near Makdadev, more than fifty kilometres from Udaipur. Rev. Daulat Masih would readily give the quarters of the CNI(Church of North India) Church for Pastor Mathews and Mary to stay whenever they visited there. Most of the time Mary accompanied her husband for doing Gospel work in the villages.

In the beginning, limited knowledge of the local language was a barrier for her to get involved in the activities. Mary possessed exceptional willpower, industrious nature and commitment, as did her husband. Therefore, instead of yielding to difficulties and challenges, she overcame them. An illustration of her fortitude unfolds in the following incident.

On the first Sunday after she reached Udaipur, following her marriage, there were only a few people in the worship service. Mary gave her testimony in Malayalam which made Pastor Mathews comment, "From next Sunday onwards, my wife will give her testimony in Hindi." Instead of refusing and commenting, she rose to the challenge. She prepared her testimony in Hindi and thoroughly memorized it. The next Sunday, complying with the wish of her husband, she gave her testimony in Hindi, much to the delight of the congregation.

She started to learn Hindi by chronologically reading the Book of Acts in the Hindustani Urdu Bible which her husband had gifted her.

She continued this habit until she could master ten words in a day. This systematic Bible reading helped her not only to learn Hindi, but also, to develop an authoritative and in-depth understanding of topics like church planting and discipleship. Moreover, the powerful presence of the Holy Spirit filled her and gently guided her.

She pursued learning the Hindi language. In 1966 itself, the year she reached Udaipur, she joined a Hindi learning course. She passed the special Hindi language test in 1968. They sung Hindi songs in family devotions. When she was studying in Bangalore, she got the opportunity to learn numerous English songs. The availability of Hindi translations of those English songs seemed a great blessing. Singing the translated Hindi versions of familiar English songs also proved to be a language learning exercise for Mary.

Today, Mary's proficiency in the language can stun anyone. She 'can write, read, sing, speak and preach fluently in Hindi.

She began her village ministry by working among children. There were many tribal children among them who used to study while staying in the government hostels. She went to work among them on Fridays and Saturdays.

There was a school at Kherwada run by Christian missionaries. Most of the children who were staying in the hostels had come there after completing their middle school education in that missionary school. Because they had already received a foundation in prayer and other spiritual matters, working among them was easy and pleasant.

The activities of Mary Mathews and her women's team deeply influenced the children. Their personalities and behaviour patterns began to reveal definite changes. The hostel warden who could not but notice the explicit transformation in the children's character, provided Mary and her team more opportunities to work for their development. As the relationship with the children became stronger, Mary and her team began to visit their villages too. The positive response from the adults in the villages resulted in the inception of a vacation Bible training centre for girls in 1970.

The course was conducted from 17th May to 30th June. Though the syllabus was designed for the girls studying in 11th and 12th standards, some grown up women also used to come and stay for a month and a half, and would leave as well trained Christians. Sisters from Rajasthan, Gujarat, Madhya Pradesh and Maharashtra came along for training.

The summer Bible school syllabus generally included topics and activities like women in the Bible, Christian family life, ministry among children, memorization of Bible verses, practice to enhance prayer life etc.

Most of the sisters who came from different places to participate in the training classes later married servants of God and are now fruitfully labouring in the vineyard of the Lord. Queena Andrews, Mrs. Michael, Sumitra Taj and Daya Cornelius are just some of them.

Besides Pennamma *Sanyasini* (a sage), Pastor M. K. Chacko and Pastor T. T. George, an array of stalwarts including Mrs. Betty Fisher from Israel, were the early teachers of the Summer Women's Bible training School.

It is worth mentioning that the honour of being the first Bible training centre for women in North India goes to the summer Bible school which functioned under the leadership of Mary Mathews.

The summer training programme continued till 1980. After that, they were compelled to discontinue the programme for want of time in the summers. By then the activities and churches of the Native Missionary Movement (NMM) had grown phenomenally and they had to devote all their time to that work.

But actually, it was not the end of a Bible training centre. Rather, it was the beginning. God upgraded the summer school that Mary Mathews had founded into a regular institute - the Filadelfia Bible College as we see it today.

# 14

# EVEN THE BUILDINGS PRAISE

When the Filadelfia Bible Institute started there were only five students! The institute took birth at Songadh in Gujarat, one of the mission fields of the Native Missionary Movement. Dr. Thomas Mathews knew that the work in north India could be sustained only through native missionaries.

In solidarity with her husband's vision, Mary too had been praying with an intense desire and spiritual burden for the initiation of a Bible training centre to train the native youths.

In 1981, when Pastor Mathews visited Muscat he got to know a brother named Thampy Mathew and upon accepting his invitation visited him at his home. As they sat there conversing, Brother Thampy said:

"If I send a small amount of money every month, will you be able to start a Bible training centre for training five North Indian youth in the Word?" "Certainly, in fact we have been praying for this matter for a while now," the pastor replied.

Thampy Mathew gave Pastor Mathews five hundred rupees and said, "This is to buy wheat flour for the students. I will send this amount every month. Let us believe that the Lord will fulfil other needs through various sources."

As soon as Pastor Mathews returned from Muscat, he started a Bible training centre in a rented room at Songadh in Gujarat with five students. The training centre was named Filadelfia Bible Institute. However, the training centre functioned there only for a year. The next year, the institute was shifted to Manohar Bhawan at 110, Chetak Marg in Udaipur.

In about one and a half years, God blessed Brother Thampy Mathew by giving him a big promotion in his job. In addition, his wife also got a good job. Following an increase in his family income, he started to send two thousand and five hundred rupees every month towards the expenses of the Bible training centre. With the increase in funds, the number of students at the centre rose from five to twenty five.

As years passed by, the number of students kept on increasing considerably. The space and facilities at Manohar Bhawan became insufficient for running the centre. Mary and Pastor Mathews kept praying for the realization of their desire to buy a plot for the construction of a building to house the Filadelfia Bible Institute.

God heard their prayer and helped them buy a two acre plot near Sanjay Park, Rani Road. A few days after the transaction, the Mathews family hosted Brother Thampy Mathew at their home. He had come to Udaipur to spend a few days with them. Before he left, he handed over eighteen thousand rupees to Pastor Mathews saying, "This is the money the Lord has entrusted me for constructing the building for the Bible institute. Let us pray! God will help us to commence the construction very soon."

On hearing this, Pastor Mathews couldn't help but laugh. He had just freed himself from the burden of debt which he had taken to buy the land. The amount of eighteen thousand rupees that he had got was just what he had in hand! The idea of constructing a building anytime soon seemed a joke. Nevertheless, he said without giving up faith:

"May God bless you! I will deposit this money in the bank. Let everything happen according to God's will!"

The very next day, he went to the bank and deposited the amount.

A few more months passed by. James Varghese, a young man who was working as a civil engineer at Banswara resigned from his job and came to Udaipur. He had reached there as a result of an inspiration from the Spirit of God that a servant of the Lord wanted to construct a four storeyed building and that he ought to support him in the construction.

A civil engineer coming to construct the four storey building! This seemed too wonderful for Pastor Mathews to even believe. The amount with them for the execution of such an enormous project was merely eighteen thousand rupees.

The young man fit the description of a complete spiritual man, stable in faith and zealous for the work of the Lord. Pastor Mathews accommodated him in his home.

Finally, construction of the building commenced with eighteen thousand rupees in hand and faith as the capital. Brother James talked with the shopkeepers familiar with him and they consented to give cement and iron rods on credit.

For the completion of the construction, every member of the church promised a month's salary and constantly prayed. As the building material was made available on credit, the construction work progressed.

Meanwhile, problems also cropped up. Many a times, severe financial crises threatened to halt the work. The shopkeepers who had lent them material came demanding money. They grew impatient as the promised date of payment was delayed again and again. Finally, there were strong manifestations of God's miraculous provisions. Several people began to extend a helping hand. When the construction work finished having overcome stiff challenges, an eighty five feet long and forty feet wide building had come up, declaring the faithfulness of God.

As the joy of seeing a big dream being fulfilled was filling the hearts, another crisis was brewing. Some employees of the Udaipur Municipal Corporation reached Filadelfia Campus and claimed that the corporation had the rights to demolish the building which they thought was illegally being constructed.

What the authorities alleged was correct. In fact, they had not taken any permission from the corporation as the site was out of its limit when the work was started. It was then a village and there was no need to take prior permission from the corporation to erect a building. It was after two years from the commencement of the work that the place came under the jurisdiction of the municipality. It seemed to be a big crisis. Rather than going for a court case, everyone fasted and prayed with a broken heart. God heard the cry of His people and spoke to Pastor Mathews as he was praying. This was the assurance he got, "Cast your cares on the LORD and He will sustain you; He will never let the righteous be shaken" (Psalm 55:22).

Pastor Mathews told those who were praying alongside him, "We don't have to fear now. The Lord will never let the righteous be shaken. He will not allow the demolition of this building"

Only four days remained for the demolition of the building as warned in the notice by the authorities. Even though, the Lord had given the promise verse, there was no idea what to do. Meanwhile, Pastor Mathews came to know that there was a Muslim official working in the office of the Municipal Corporation. He located the house of that official with difficulty and went to visit him one night. The official had also heard that a building belonging to Christians was going to be demolished in the near future.

"Sir, you must help us in this crisis situation," Pastor Mathews pleaded.

"How can I help you people, when you have acted unlawfully?" The officer replied. He was not willing to help them.

"If we submit an application in the proper way, your office will never grant us the sanction. In that case, we won't be able to build. If the sanction is denied once, we know our hands will be tied forever. That is why we erected the building. We believe God will work for us" replied Pastor Mathews.

The officer couldn't help but laugh hearing what Pastor Mathews said. He asked, "How can God help you in such a situation?"

Pastor Mathews learned that the officer was a staunch Muslim, so he said, "Sir, do you know that this building has been constructed with the help of the donations received from hundreds of believers. Numerous believers have given their contributions towards buying the land, construction of the building and other things. Now, we are praying for the survival of the building. You also believe in God. You too believe in *Isa* (meaning Jesus in the Urdu language). *Isa* is your prophet too. Hence, you should help us with regard to this building which has been built in the name of *Nabi Isa* (meaning Prophet Jesus)."

God worked in the heart of that officer and he said, "I don't know whether I can do anything. Anyhow, if there is anything which I can do, I will indeed do it."

The next day the officer came to see the building. He went up to the terrace along with Pastor Mathews. It was the most beautiful building in that area. The elegance struck the officer; moreover, it was a house of prayer where people gathered in the name of *Nabi Isa*. In the wake of the realization that such a building was going to be demolished, that government officer seemed to be in great mental strife.

As he walked up and down seemingly having lost the calm of his mind, he noticed a date scribbled on the wall in a corner and asked, "What is that date?"

"That I had scribbled with my fingers on the day of the roofing," Mathews replied.

"Are you telling the truth?" he asked excitedly.

"Yes… I scribbled it when the cement was still wet," replied Mathews.

That officer took out the order of demolition from his file. After reading it repeatedly, he said aloud, "What a wonder! Your prayer to *Nabi Isa* has been heard. There is a huge difference between the date you have scribbled in cement and the date in this demolition order. The order has to be issued before the date of the roofing, at least, ten days in advance."

The rule regarding demolition of a building was that if authorities wanted to demolish a building or stop the construction, they had to send the notice ten days before the roofing of that building was done. Once the roofing had been done, even the government did not possess the power or authority to demolish the building.

"It is a setback for our office. The date typed in the order is post the roofing of your building. Actually, the Municipal Corporation officials had taken the decision to demolish the building long back. But, the typist erred while entering the date. Now, nobody can demolish your church building. All things are in your favour," the officer explained.

The last date for the demolition also passed. Nothing happened. Later, all the four storeys were completed as per the original plan. Today it is a complex with various facilities like class rooms of the Bible College, dormitory for boys, FBC library and the office of the Native Missionary Movement, standing tall as a testimony to the work of God. In front of the building, a church hall was also constructed with a seating capacity of one thousand. At that point of time, there was no other Pentecostal church hall in North India with such a huge capacity.

The headquarters of the Filadelfia Fellowship of Churches have grabbed the attention of the global Christian community remaining a symbol of the glory of the living God and the sign of the dedication and hard work of the missionary couple, Mary and Thomas Mathews. Indeed the building today is a sign of God's faithful provision for His people.

# 15

---

# A DOOR THAT NO ONE CAN SHUT

In the year 1975, the then Prime Minister Mrs. Indira Gandhi declared the state of emergency in India under article 352. The national emergency was one of the most controversial and tumultuous periods in Indian politics.

Mrs. Gandhi imprisoned almost all leaders belonging to the opposition parties. The imprisoned leaders formed the Janta Party inside the jail.

The party was a confluence of Bharatiya Jana Sangh, Socialist Party, Congress (O), Charan Singh's Bharatiya Lok Dal and many other parties. In the subsequent general elections of 1977, Indira Gandhi had to concede defeat to the Janata Party. For the first time ever in the Indian political history, Congress became a minority in the parliament. On 24th March, the Janta government assumed power with Morarji Desai as the Prime Minister.

As the Indian politics passed through turbulent times, the church of God in India was also facing many odds. The trial by fire came in the second year of Morarji's reign. Janta party's Member of Parliament, Mr. Om Prakash Tyagi, presented a bill in the parliament which if passed and implemented would pose tough challenges to the advent of Christianity in India. The bill was entitled the 'Freedom of Religion' Bill. Though the word 'freedom' was mentioned in the name of the bill, O. P. Tyagi's bill contained numerous primitive clauses which sought to violate all freedom of the Christians in India.

Tyagi's bill was a revised version of the Anti-conversion Law implemented in Orissa in 1967, in Madhya Pradesh in 1968 and in Arunachal Pradesh in 1977 by the Congress governments in those states. At one stage, the probability of the bill being passed in the parliament became strong. The looming threat shook the Christian community. Like many other leaders of the Christian organisations serving in India, the missionary couple Mary and Thomas Mathews also lost their sleep during those anxious days and nights. The notion that the doors for the Gospel in India were going to close, prevailed everywhere.

## The Navapur Story

Pastor Mathews felt an urge in the Spirit to fast and pray for a few days in the wake of such a development. But it was not easy to fast staying in Udaipur because of the constant inflow of people and guests in his home. As he contemplated about it, a good idea occurred to him – pray and fast while staying at Pai village, a place located about 30 kilometres away from Udaipur.

Without any delay he left for Pai. There he spent time in the presence of God fasting, praying and meditating on the Word of God along with his disciple Tajendra Masih. On the tenth day of the fast, God spoke to Pastor Mathews through a scripture:

"I know your deeds. See, I have placed before you an open door that no one can shut. I know that you have little strength, yet you have kept my word" (Revelation 3: 18).

Besides, he received a vision in which he saw the map of Western India; he himself was going along with some brothers towards that zone. With God communing with him through the Word and the vision, he felt convinced that it was time to stop the fast. When Pastor Mathews conveyed to Mary the Word and the vision, she felt great joy and relief; because, she knew it was a confirmation from God. Those days, while she was praying she had also perceived that the doors were not closing, but rather, they were opening up for the Gospel.

Pastor Mathews scoured numerous shops in Udaipur for the particular map that he had seen in the vision, but, he could not find one. Finally, a brother from the Church of North India who was working with the Railways told him that he could get the zonal map from the Railway Training Institute. He went there along with Brother Vishwas and to his pleasant surprise he found there the same map which he had seen in the vision. A railway employee gave him the map.

Pastor Mathews shared his vision with his church in Udaipur and other fellow brothers. All of them started to pray focusing on the vision. Once during a prayer meeting held at the house of Brother M. Philip at Bhupalpura, his wife Elizabeth brought a plate in the midst of all those assembled there and said: "Now, we are going to take an offering for the fulfilment of the vision God has given to our Pastor. Those who are willing can contribute financially and put your offering into this plate." Saying this, she put into the vessel whatever amount she had in her hand. After that, everyone who had come there for the meeting gave as they could. Finally when they counted the money it added up to four hundred and thirty rupees.

Pastor Mathews and his disciple Tajendra Masih, along with three other brothers, set out for the interior village of Raniamba in Gujarat. All they had for their travelling and other expenses were the four hundred and thirty rupees received as an offering in that house. There was a special reason behind their journey to Raniamba. As the pastor and the team of five prepared to leave for the place he had seen in the vision, he received a letter from Nandurbar district in Maharashtra. The letter read:

"I have seen the song book that you published. I want to buy one too, but I don't have anything to pay towards its cost. I will appreciate if you will send it to me. I will be here in this hostel until the end of April. If you are sending it after that then, please, send it to my village address. My house is in Raniamba near Songadh in Gujarat."

The sender of the letter was a girl named Ruth. That was the only address they had that guided their journey into the place that God showed in the vision. Enquiries regarding the location of their destination yielded the information that Raniamba was five kilometres further off Songadh in Southern Gujarat and no bus plied to that place. They began their journey and by evening, the team reached Songadh and reached the village on foot carrying their luggage on their heads. They made enquiries about the address given in the letter. But, Ruth was not there.

There the pastor and his team struck up a conversation with a middle-aged man sitting in front of a small hut. They introduced themselves to him as evangelists from Rajasthan who had come there inspired by God in a special manner. On hearing that, the man whose name was Gorjibhai stood up and praised God, raising both his hands. He embraced Pastor Mathews and the brethren with him, and welcomed them to his home. Then, he told them about the vision he had seen a few weeks earlier, "The voice of God told me in my dream that five servants of God would come from Rajasthan carrying their luggage on their heads, and I should receive them into my home and learn the Word of God from them." He paused for a moment before adding excitedly, "All these days, I have been expecting you here."

When they thought about the plans and arrangements of Almighty God, they praised and glorified Him.

On the subsequent days Pastor Mathews and his team continuously conducted meetings in that village. God's saving grace manifested through His awesome deeds and many people turned to the living God.

After three weeks, Pastor Mathews and the brothers returned to Udaipur, and Mary Mathews and her eight-member-women team took over from where they had left. They stayed in the huts and spread divine radiance in the spiritual, physical and social realms of the people living there. During the three weeks of their stay, Mary and her team ministered to the local community in diverse simple ways possible. Their mode of work proved an effective paradigm of evangelism.

Most of the families in the village were in distress because of the alcoholism and indiscipline of the men folk. In such a context, the despondent women got attracted to Christianity, to the path of love and peace. The conversion of a woman from a family led to the salvation of the whole family.

Mary and the team worked in the villages throughout the day and as the sun would set, the rural women would receive them as guests into their houses in the hamlets with walls made of bamboo strips woven together, plastered with glutinous mud. The simple women welcomed them with open hearts into their humble houses, served them food and gave them a place to sleep. They used to lie on the floor spreading any piece of cloth or mat available.

In the morning, the rural women would take Mary and the rest of the team to the homes of the sick people in the area. Wherever they went they would share the Gospel of Jesus and then pray for the healing of the sick and the fulfilment of the other needs. Thus they travelled through the villages during the daytime and formed a strong relationship with everyone. The women, children and men they met during the day would come to the open air meeting held during the night. These spiritual meetings led to lives being changed and people receiving Christ into their hearts. Churches were planted among the villagers who were thus reformed spiritually and socially. The team was able to set a historical pattern of ministry without even being aware of it.

## The Madhya Pradesh Story

In a similar manner, in 1988, Mary toured Jhabua and Alirajpur in Madhya Pradesh, along with a women's team for two months. They also carried a film projector and tracts with them. They went from village to village screening the film. Many people turned to the Lord and a church planting movement was thus initiated. Later other servants of God also went there and consolidated the work. Several young men from that region came to be trained at the Bible College in Udaipur. They returned after graduating and have planted over a hundred native churches. The fire of revival is still spreading through the region.

At a time when it seemed that the 'Freedom of Religion Bill' introduced by O. P. Tyagi would be passed in the parliament, Mary and Pastor Mathews, along with several other children of God, knelt down in the presence of God and prayed that the doors of the Gospel would not close in India. The doors did not close at all but rather they opened wider still! The organization which had been confined only to Rajasthan with the name Rajasthan Pentecostal Church (RPC) expanded to the neighbouring state of Gujarat. Later it spread to several other states too and the churches thus planted were named the Filadelfia Fellowship Churches of India.

# 16

# IMPRINTS OF COURAGE

**M**ary comes across as an outstanding personality in the sphere of Indian evangelism. Her contributions are entirely different in their nature and dimension. She possesses remarkable intellect and a spirit of adventure which can even take men by surprise. It is not strange that we can notice the same spiritual qualities and characteristics in most of the women who worked closely with her since the early stages of her missionary life. Here are a few of those women.

## Anandibai

The history of Pandita Ramabai is also the history of the resurgence of women. The credit of taking the pioneering steps in different social sectors for the upliftment of women duly goes to her. It was she who initiated the educational and welfare schemes for the widows in India. She constantly worked for the absolute emancipation and upliftment of women across India. The inspiration for her to work for the marginalized and the oppressed came from Jesus Christ who had given meaning to her life.

She searched for God in all religions. Though, she was able to find some good ideas in all religions, she could not find a saviour. Ultimately, when she found Jesus Christ, she found everything she had been searching for. She founded the Mukti Mission on 11th March, 1889 as a platform to utilise the knowledge and light she had thus attained.

Anandibai who took active participation in the missionary activities of Mary was a girl brought up at the Mukti Mission. When she grew up she was married off to a man from Banswara, in southern Rajasthan. Although she had lived in the fullness of the Spirit, at the Mukti Mission she was passing through a state of spiritual dryness. That was when Pastor Mathews went there with one of his associates, Brother Samson Wilson and took a small room in an inn to stay and started to preach the Word of God. This resulted in the spiritual revival of Anandibai.

Valu Singh, Patras Masih, Tajendra Masih and others who were students staying in the hostel came into the experience of salvation. Entrusting the work in that city to Samson Wilson, Pastor Mathews returned to Udaipur.

During a Christmas vacation in Banswara, when Anandibai who had come from the Mukti Mission was the warden of the ladies hostel at the Mission Compound, the Holy Spirit swept over the students who were worshipping. They began to speak in other tongues. The students thus filled with the Holy Spirit experienced the strange phenomenon of not being able to speak what they wished to speak when they opened their mouths because words in other tongues came out.

Anandibai was a student in the first batch of the women's summer Bible school, which Mary had started for girls. Although she had completed her training in the first year, she would keep coming back every year with other girls and stay there for weeks labouring for the successful organisation of the classes.

Anandibai was like the mother of Rufus seen in the Bible (Mark 15: 21). Her name and presence were inconspicuous. But silently yet zealously, she worked for the expansion of the Kingdom.

## Sheila Kamble

Janardhan Kamble, a native of Maharashtra, was the owner of a fabrication company in Mumbai. He was an affluent person but also an alcoholic. Once he came to Udaipur in connection with some fabrication work. One Sunday afternoon when Pastor Mathews and a few brothers from the church were riding bicycles to reach nearby villages with the Gospel, Janardhan Kamble and his friends were seen enjoying themselves in a park.

When Kamble heard the men singing Christian songs, he clapped his hands to catch their attention and said to them, "I heard you singing. Can you sing a song for us also?"

Pastor Mathews' team stood under that tree by the wayside and sang a Hindi song, praising the living God. Kamble and his companions returned the favour by singing a song of their choice! They hilariously sang a cinema song!!

But before parting, Pastor Mathews wrote his address on a tiny piece of paper and handing it over to Kamble, invited him for a Sunday worship service. Normally, nobody would say no to the invitation for a worship service. People used to say that they would certainly come, but, would conveniently forget about it then and there. But, Janardhan Kamble was a different person. The very next Sunday he came over in his car along with his workers at the right time. He attended the worship service with total devotion and awe. He experienced a tranquillity and joy as never before. In the subsequent weeks, Kamble came again for worship without fail and a big change started to take place in his heart. Gradually and to his surprise, he completely gave up alcohol and never turned back again. Within a short while he gave his heart to Jesus and later received water baptism.

What everyone saw after that was the fire of evangelism flaring up in the devout Kamble. He began to go with the church's team for the

Gospel work in his car. He bought a brand new mike set and gifted it to the church.

In between, he went back to Mumbai and brought his wife and children. He wanted them to know this Jesus who had changed his life. When they arrived they could not believe the change that they saw. His wife and children too embraced the faith and took water baptism and began to grow in Christ.

Like Janardhan, fondly called Kamble *sahab,* his wife Sheila Kamble also had the large-heartedness to do anything, anytime to extend the borders of the Kingdom of God.

The Kamble family took Pastor Mathews and Mary in their car to Mumbai, Pune, Kedgaon, Ahmednagar and Sakri providing them with opportunities to preach the Gospel extensively. Once, when one of his construction projects was underway in Goa, he took Pastor Mathews there to ensure that everyone working for him heard the Gospel.

The business of Janardhan Kamble meanwhile was not doing that good. And then after a few years he was diagnosed with cancer to which he later succumbed. A few years later, Sister Sheila Kamble was also diagnosed with cancer. They lost their wealth and position; but the vicissitudes of life did not affect their spiritual lives at all. Sister Sheila Kamble and her family had a broad vision and huge burden for souls in their home state Maharashtra. It was Sister Sheila Kamble who introduced the 'Zarephath Jar,' boxes that were distributed to the homes of believers, where they could save money regularly to give towards the Filadelfia Bible College ministries.

Every year Sister Sheila Kamble comes to the Navapur Convention with a gift offering of small and big contributions from various places for organising the convention.

It might be God's commission and justice that Sangeeta Awale, the daughter of the couple Sheila and Janardhan, who carried the dream of the spiritual revival of Maharashtra in their hearts, has been the chief worship leader of Navapur Convention, held on Maharashtra's soil and is the largest revival meeting in North India, for some years now. Sangeeta's husband is a medical doctor in Mumbai; after spending only a few hours in the clinic, he devotes the rest of the time to carry out Gospel activities in slum areas and other places.

Even today, Sheila Kamble and her family have only one prayer-Maharashtra should know Christ.

## Mrs. D. P. Roy

Mrs. D. P. Roy made a significant contribution in the life and ministry of Mary at one time.

When Mary was living with her family in a small rented house in Udaipur, Mrs. Roy who retired as the District Educational Officer (DEO) too lived in the same building. She was of great help to Mary's family. Whenever Mary left for a long duration in connection with the Gospel work, she would leave her children under the care of Mrs. Roy.

Mary and Mrs. Roy came to know each other when the latter once came to attend a ten-day prayer meeting at the Gospel Centre. Gradually, their acquaintance developed into a very intimate friendship. Mrs. Roy keenly attended the Bible studies conducted at the Gospel Centre.

At that time, there were two Malaysian students studying at the Udaipur University College. Both of them attended the worship services at the Gospel Centre. One of them, named Nathaniel, was the son of a Methodist pastor and he knew Mrs. Roy. It was through him that she came to the Gospel Centre and struck an acquaintance with Mary.

As activities and the organization expanded, on many occasions it became necessary to contact different government departments for various matters. Mrs. Roy, being a retired government servant, was of considerable help and influence.

Mrs. Roy's contribution and help was one of the factors that encouraged Pastor Mathews to leap into the educational sector. The history of the St. Mathews School, hugely popular in Udaipur and its outskirts for its academic excellence and various other accomplishments, and the Modern School at Dungarpur, run by Pastor K. O. Varghese, the General Secretary of the Filadelfia Fellowship, also owes a lot to the inspiration provided by Mrs. D.P. Roy.

## Sardaribai

The students of the Filadelfia Bible College used to go to the villages for weekend ministry on Friday evenings and Saturdays.

Once when they went to a village named Gujjar, they visited the house of Heeralal who was bedridden and was unable to even do his daily routines because of his paralysis.

The Bible college students shared with Mary, the miseries which the bedridden man was suffering in the interior village, with his wife and five children. She was deeply moved by his plight. Hearing the sad state of this family she decided to go and meet them. She went to Gujjar along with some brothers from the church and the Bible college students, and stayed there overnight.

Hard work was needed for the sustenance of the family. Heeralal lay helpless trying to suppress the severe pain as he watched his wife bear the burden of the family all alone. Their parents and brethren deserted them as they saw the deteriorating condition of Heeralal, without any hope of recovery.

Despite the adverse circumstances and the bitterness of desertion by relatives, Sardari had been taking care of her husband with full devotion. She did not murmur even once rather one could never see her without a smile on her face. As her husband was bedridden, she took up the hard tasks on the farm like tilling the land, normally done only by men, besides doing all the household chores. She did all the work undeterred.

Looking at Sardari, Mary was reminded of the wedding vows, "...for better or for worse, for richer or for poorer, in sickness and in health, to love, cherish, and to obey, till death us do part... "

Lying helpless on that bed of pain, Heeralal accepted the Lord Jesus Christ as his Saviour. Afterwards, he attended the Bible study classes conducted at Makadadev. God filled him with the spirit of wisdom. Though bedridden, he continuously read the Bible.

Taking everyone by surprise, after a while, Heeralal asked to be immersed in baptism even though he was lying flat on a bed.

One day one of the students, Ankur Masih suggested to Mary, "Aunty, let us take Heeralal to Udaipur!" "It is right. If we unceasingly pray for this brother, God will work," Mary replied with faith.

A few days later, Sardari brought Heeralal to Udaipur. She was pushing him in a push cart as she brought him to the Filadelfia campus!

When Mary saw that sight, she could not believe her eyes. But they decided to pray for Heeralal's healing.

Under the leadership of Ankur Masih, the Bible college students became alert and active in taking care of Heeralal. They nursed him sincerely. They used to bathe him every afternoon after giving him a mustard oil massage. And everyone kept praying for him. Changes became visible on his face within two days. In between, a neurologist examined him and said:

"A surgery can be done. But there is not much hope."

Finally, the surgery was conducted as advised by the doctor. What a miracle! The surgery turned out to be a great success; even, the doctor could not believe it! Spinal tumour was the cause of his sickness. Heeralal, slowly but steadily, returned to a life of normalcy.

Heeralal who was brought lying in a push cart went back after four months walking on his own feet with a broad smile lit on his face.

Today, Heeralal is the pastor of a growing church in the same village, Gujjar. Whenever, Mary sees his wife Sardari, she cannot thank God enough for His faithfulness and also Sardari for her love for Heeralal.

# 17

# MANIFESTATION OF AN AWAKENING

On 14th January, 1994, a phenomenal manifestation of the Holy Spirit started to take place in the Vineyard Church near Pearson Airport in Toronto, Canada.

The revival that originated in Toronto began to spread to the churches all over the world in the subsequent days. Thousands of people started to visit the Vineyard Church, known today as the Airport Christian Fellowship. Hundreds of thousands of pastors also came and participated in the meetings at the Vineyard Church to catch the flames of revival. The experiences of unceasing laughter, incessant crying, shivering, falling or resting in the Spirit and other visible manifestations.

The winds of the Toronto Revival blew strongly into the Filadelfia campus in Udaipur on 17th June 1995 while a three – day youth camp was underway. Most of the participants were from Udaipur with the exception of four or five participants from Abu Road, Dungarpur, Jodhpur and Jaipur.

That day, the participants experienced a flow of the Spirit on the first day of the camp itself, a Friday. Brother Edi Okoro from Nigeria was the main speaker. He taught from the Bible with total authenticity. An increasing hunger and thirst for the presence of God became apparent in the youth as they listened to the word of God. Later that day, all of them together took a decision: to tarry for the experiences and anointing of the Holy Spirit the next day i.e. Saturday.

The meeting began in the morning. As the meeting progressed, the presence of the Holy Spirit grew stronger. And finally a stage reached which could have been literally described as the explosion or downpour of the Spirit.

There formed a river of the Spirit, first ankle-deep, then knee-deep, then up to the waist, and finally over the head, that it could not be crossed as seen in Ezekiel 47: 4 & 5. All the youth who congregated there on that day swam in that river of the Spirit, unmindful of whatsoever situations they were in. On that single day, more than thirty five young people were filled with the Holy Spirit and began to speak in other tongues.

Pastor Mathews was then on a tour to the United States of America. When he made a phone call to Udaipur sometime in between, Mary informed him about the revival that was then taking place among the youth who were attending the camp. When he heard the news, he was filled with great joy, because both of them had been incessantly praying for such an experience those days.

Hearing about the revival taking place among the youth in the church, it aroused Pastor Mathews' curiosity. He asked Mary to call his son Paul so that he could get more information from him about the revival. But, Mary told him that he could not be brought to the phone as he was lying inside the hall 'slain in the Spirit.' When Pastor Mathews called again, to speak to his son, Paul, who was a college student at that time, was still lying on the floor slain.

When that revival was taking place, Paul was only twenty years old. The exposure to the power of the Holy Spirit he had in the midst of the revival became a turning point in his life.

Paul Mathews who holds a doctorate in Psychology from the Mohanlal Sukhadia University (erstwhile Udaipur University) does not consider his academic qualification or his ancestry the strength behind his ministries. Because, what transformed him from an ordinary, introvert and a shy youth, to a pastor with extraordinary charisma, just as we see him today, was nothing else but the fire of the Holy Spirit that had leapt high on the Filadelfia campus on the 17th of July, 1995.

The youth camp was to conclude with the night meeting at 9pm, followed by dinner. But, the wind of the Holy Spirit which had started to blow in the morning was still blowing without a pause even during the night. All the youth kept swimming in the river of the Spirit that night. They continued rejoicing in the presence of God impervious to physical hunger or thirst. Though dinner was prepared for everyone, nobody had it since all were filled with the presence of the Holy Spirit.

As we read in Romans 14: 17, "For the kingdom of God is not a matter of eating and drinking but of righteousness and peace and joy in the Holy Spirit." What happened there at that time was the visible manifestation of the Holy Spirit.

The next day being Sunday, everyone came to the worship service. The meeting started exactly at 8 am with prayer. The revival which broke out in the youth camp the previous day repeated itself in the Sunday service as well. Pastor John C. Varghese who is spearheading the ministries of the Filadelfia Fellowship Church in Orissa now, was the worship leader that Sunday. He started singing a Hindi song "Daud kay nai, nachtey nachtey, Abba ki stuti karoonga." (Like David, I will dance and praise Abba the Father).

The entire church sang together. With closed eyes, hands raised towards heaven, all kept singing and rejoicing in the Holy Spirit, forgetting themselves and oblivious to their surroundings. By the second time that the song was being repeated, people were being filled with the Holy Spirit in the hall. People lost sense of where they were and began to jump and dance in the Spirit. The service that began at 8 am went on till 12.30 p.m., but it seemed like only a few minutes to all the worshippers. This revival led a few youngsters, including Paul Mathews to commit their lives to Jesus. Several of them are still in the mainstream of the Rajasthan Pentecostal Church, being fruitfully used in the hands of the Lord in different capacities.

The revival in Udaipur spread to various places in Rajasthan and touched numerous people from diverse backgrounds.

Prominent revival historian, Dr. J. Edwin Orr has repeated a comment in the introduction to all his books in the series Evangelical Awakenings: "There is the possibility that an awakening may be restricted to a single place; at the same time, an awakening has the potential to spread its flame to the whole world." Orr was revealing a historical fact when he wrote this.

While perusing the history of awakenings, it is not seen that all awakenings were welcomed by all people. In different parts of the world, several revivals would have taken place, which were suppressed before they could make it into the annals of history.

Why do awakenings get suppressed? The reason may be the lack of appropriate study on the topic of revivals. We can presume that in the absence of a clear cognizance or perception of revival, one tends to evaluate revivals on the basis of prejudices in one's mind which naturally stunt the advent of awakening.

We must have a clear understanding of the reality. It is not necessary that all the revivals should be homogenous. For example, when revival broke out in Toronto, the revived believers began to laugh in a spontaneous and uncontrollable manner whereas during the awakening in the Udaipur Church, school and college students repented in the presence of God, remembering their sins and lay on the floor crying.

Whatever may be the external demonstration(s), revival means the reformation of individuals and or society. Mere external demonstrations without reformation can only be termed as counterfeit awakenings or emotional demonstrations. They vanish in a short span of time.

History gives us no evidence of revivals being manifested through individuals delimiting the scope of the Holy Spirit's works and underestimating His power. If the lives of George Whitefield, John Wesley and Jonathan Edwards have become merged with the history of revivals, it was because of the fact that they had yearned and lived for limitless works of the Holy Spirit.

The revival in Udaipur too was manifested in the midst of a group of school and college students mentored by the missionary couple Pastor and Mary Mathews, who removed every obstacle that would have restricted the work of God.

# 18

# NAVAPUR CONVENTION: A SMALL BEGINNING

Navapur is a municipality and a headquarter for Navapur *taluka* (an administrative district comprising of a number of villages) in Maharashtra. It is situated at a distance of approximately 110 km from Surat city in Gujarat. The Rangavaly river flows by Navapur. The railway station of Navapur is built in two states; one half of it is in Maharashtra and the other half is in Gujarat. It is an interesting fact that even a train which halts at Navapur Railway station is stationed half in Maharashtra and half in Gujarat.

Navapur is also a thriving marketing and processing town for the surrounding agricultural areas. There are agro based industries such as a sugar factory and a *tuvar dal* (kind of a split pulse) mill as well as other food processing facilities in the municipality. The town is also famous for animal husbandry and poultry farming. The *tuvar dal* which grows profusely on the tribal farms without the use of fertilisers and insecticides is a speciality belonging to Navapur.

The nearest commercial airport is in Surat. The average literacy rate in Navapur is 67%, higher than the national average of 59.5% with male literacy at 72%, and female literacy at 62%.

These are some bright spots in the development story of Navapur. But the history of the place was filled with darkness. The yesterdays of this place would tell the story of the insults and trauma suffered by the tribal people who were living on the margins of society, deserted by all, without even being considered humans, and deprived of their rights and privileges. The sad part was that they were not even aware of what they could get or not get.

The tribal hutments were once worse than hell with rampant gambling and spurious liquor dominating the lives of the people. Even the women used to distill arrack and drink liquor. Hunger and the resultant brawls, tussles and mugging were common incidents. Superstitions and evil practices dragged this community further backwards. Gamit, Vasave and Mavchi are the chief tribes in Navapur. The arrival of a woman named Mary Mathews into the midst of semi naked, primitive tribes and the subsequent events became astonishing chapters in history!

In the month of December, 1980, Mary and Mrs. Masih were stationed in Raniamba in Gujarat, travelling to the adjacent villages and sharing the Gospel with the rural and tribal people. One of those days, some patients from the backward district of Dangs were brought to them for prayer. As they prayed, all the patients were healed instantly. As a result, they got the opportunity to go to some more villages with the Gospel. Thus, they went to Golan village near Subeer with some villagers. They stayed in that village for three days; they visited houses and conducted public meetings. People came from the surrounding villages to attend those meetings. After receiving a message from home, they decided to cut down on the number of meetings and return to Udaipur.

Mary and Mrs. Masih boarded the Ahwa – Navapur bus and reached Navapur. When they reached, they learnt that there were two buses between 4 o' clock and 5 o' clock that would bring them to Surat, the big bus station from where they could get buses to reach Udaipur. The wait for the 4 o' clock bus turned futile as they later learnt that the bus had broken down on the way. The second bus did not halt at Navapur as it was already jam-packed with passengers. As they stood there not knowing what to do next, someone told them that if they went to Uchchal, some distance away, they would get a bus. They walked fast to that place carrying their bags and reached there by 7 o' clock in the evening. Though they waited there till 8.30 pm, they did not get any bus to Surat.

As darkness fell, the place where they stood and its surroundings became desolate. Mrs. Masih grew tense thinking about where to go to find shelter along with a thirty one–year–old young woman, Mary. They were in a strange place and it was a dark night. It was an anxious ordeal to wait there.

They bought two cups of tea from a nearby tea stall. Actually they had no real desire to have tea, but they went to the stall with the intention of getting to know someone who might offer them help. As they paid the stall owner, they disclosed their helplessness to him. Immediately he pointed towards a family standing there and said, "Look there! It is a Christian family standing there. If you go to them they will indeed help you."

With fast steps, they walked expectantly towards the family. After the introductions were done, the desperate women learnt that they were talking to Ratna Master and family, travelling missionaries of the Alliance Mission. Ratna Master was a devout evangelist who played the harmonium while ministering.

When he heard that they were stranded in that place unable to travel further, he told them, "There is no use standing here. You won't get any vehicle. We are going to *Nathal Bhajan Mandali* (a special Christmas gathering) in the village of Patti Bandra in Nijar *Taluka*, which is far from here. You come along with us. In the morning we will get you on board the bus."

It seemed to Mary and Mrs. Masih that the members of the missionary family standing before them were angels sent by God to help them find their way.

They reached village Patti Bandra before 10 o' clock that night.

More than five hundred people had gathered there from the villages near and far. Mary and Mrs. Masih who reached there unexpectedly, were accorded a warm welcome. They had dinner comprising rice and dal. That night both of them spoke from the word of God thrice.

After every message, the gathering would break into a song and worship. Thus alternating between messages and songs, they spent the whole night in the presence of God.

In the morning, a person named William Master came to Mary, who was all set to leave for Udaipur, and said, "Our meetings are scheduled at various places these days. The messages of God heard from you were a blessing to all of us. So, please, be with us for a few more days."

In those days when there was no internet, email or cellular phone, leaving her little children behind in Udaipur, Mary, the brilliant woman missionary, persisted with the evangelistic assignment, the Lord had entrusted to her, travelling in Gujarat, Maharashtra and Madhya Pradesh, and staying in the Adivasi tribal huts accepting whatever they gave as food.

In 1981, Mary came to the house of William Masters' daughter, Chotibai, at Karanji Khurd village near Navapur. Staying there she actively worked in the adjacent villages. That family had much financial constraints then, but, they happily hosted Mary at their home.

Those days, there was only a small fellowship of twenty five people at Karanji Khurd.

It was then that Kanti Behan built a new house at Navihonda. In connection with the dedication of the newly built house, a prayer meeting was arranged in front of the house. A lot of people came and attended the meeting which was the first Christian public gathering in that place. In the meeting, Mary ministered powerfully from the Word of God. Many accepted the Lord Jesus Christ as their Saviour. Mary worked in Navihonda and Karanji Khurd and the surrounding villages, leading to the salvation of a large number of people. On one of the following days, Mary sent a telegram to her husband, Pastor Mathews. He and his team came from Udaipur and baptized people who received Christ as their Saviour during those meetings. History does not end with the aforesaid series of events in 1980; it was actually the beginning.

And what a beginning it was! During his visit in 1980, Pastor Mathews, along with Mary, conducted a small Gospel meeting at the Government Lower Primary school in the village of Karanji Khurd near Navapur. The gathering was not very big, only a handful of people were there. As there was no power supply, the meetings were conducted in the dim light of a few lanterns.

This meeting was held every subsequent year without a break. As years passed by, the number of participants also went up. God's work began to be increasingly revealed year after year. The sick were healed and scores of people were delivered from demonic oppression.

As the meeting grew in magnitude, miracles, signs and wonders became the hallmark of the convention.

That small Gospel meeting, which was started by Pastor Mathews and Mary at the Karanji Khurd Government Lower Primary School in the dim light of a lantern has grown now into the popular 'Navapur Convention' as we know it today!

This confluence of multitudes famously known as the Navapur Convention is the general convention of the Filadelfia Fellowship of Churches with its headquarters in Udaipur. More than being the annual national convention of the Filadelfia Church, it comes alive as the spiritual festival of the whole land.

The number of people participating in the convention has been increasing every year. In spite of the huge flow of multitude to the venue, the discipline at this large festival event is remarkable.

The curtain comes down on the convention with the Sunday worship service and the Holy Communion. While mentioning Navapur, the name of Pastor Panthu Bhai cannot be forgotten. Pantu Bhai who was the pastor of the Filadelfia church in Karanji Khurd fulfilled his ministry successfully being the leader of that entire area too.

Karanji Khurd and the people there are an example of the extent to which the Gospel of Jesus Christ can influence and transform individuals and society. Once upon a time, the people were illiterate and primitive. But now among young men and women of the current generation there are highly educated post graduates and professional degree holders. It is only because of the Gospel that they are occupying the mainstream of the society with their heads held high. The people of the village have surged ahead in education and culture as well as socially and spiritually.

Every year since 1981, which was the inaugural year of the Navapur Convention, till now, the gentle presence of Mary Mathews has been visible to all.

# 19

# TO LOVE, CHERISH AND OBEY

One thing that Pastor Mathews had been repeatedly trying to tell his wife Mary since January, 2005, was to shift their residence from Udaipur to Navapur. But, Mary was not at all happy to hear even the suggestion of moving to Navapur. The reason being she was anxious about the health of her husband.

Because of his constant journeys without enough rest, Pastor Mathews had developed acute asthma. Pastor Thomas and Mary Mathews had arrived in the city of Houston in the United States of America to take part in a missionary conference in April, 1990. After the conference, they ministered in meetings arranged by some well-wishers. Thereafter, Mary returned to India by the end of May. Pastor Mathews stayed back and continued ministering. He reached the house of Brother M. C. Jacob as his guest. After dining and praying together, he went upstairs retiring for the day.

A short while after he lay down, his asthmatic condition began to trouble him. The intensity of the trouble increased with each passing moment. The asthma had become very severe by 4 o' clock in the morning and he fell down on the floor as he tried to walk to the washroom. When Brother M. C. Jacob and his wife came up and looked, his body had turned cold and blue. Immediately, the ambulance was called and he was taken to the hospital. There he received highly specialized treatment. He regained consciousness only after half an hour and gradually became normal again. It was the subsequent check-up that revealed the condition of his heart; he had cardio-myopathy.

The doctor who evaluated his physical condition asked him to slow down. But, the zealous evangelist in him turned down the expert medical advice even though his health had deteriorated over the years.

Just before the Navapur Convention in 2005, Pastor Mathews had to preach in the conventions in Anand, Gujarat and in Nagpur, Maharashtra. For health reasons, his son Dr. Paul Mathews accompanied him on his journey to Nagpur.

The doctor had said, "The more you rest, the longer you will live." Pastor Mathews was unhappy to hear this news from his doctor since he wanted to travel and preach the good news of Jesus. He used to say, "My call is for evangelism. If I am unable to do that what use do I have of a long life?"

As Mary was anxious for his health, she sincerely hoped that her husband might cut down on his journeys and preaching as far as possible, and instead devote more time to writing books and articles. His decision to shift to Navapur worried her very much.

Whenever Pastor Mathews tried to raise the topic of shifting to Navapur, Mary consciously avoided it. She knew he was adamant in his decisions. Pastor Mathews might have felt that Mary was intentionally evading the topic of shifting to Navapur. In the midst of a Sunday worship service in the month of March, 2005, he announced his desire and vision publicly in the church:

## Chapter 19

"I am not burdened about the Udaipur church any more. You all have grown up; even if I don't live here permanently anymore, it will not affect you adversely in any manner. I will keep coming here in between. In a short while, I am shifting to Navapur. I don't know whether my wife will come along with me. Whether she follows me or not, I will be leaving this place."

When he was leaving just as he had announced publicly, Mary was with him. In spite of all that Mary wanted to do, she consistently ensured that she obeyed Pastor Mathews.

A building which was previously used for poultry farming had already been hired for them to lodge after shifting to Navapur. After reaching Navapur they shifted part of their belongings and began a new chapter in their life. For three months after their arrival in Navapur, they continuously travelled, preaching and proclaiming the Gospel in every nook and corner of that area.

But, by the end of June, Mary's fear came true; Pastor Mathews fell sick.

Mary along with Biju and Rajni, brought Pastor Mathews to the doctor at Chinchpada Mission Hospital. The doctor remarked after examining him:

"You cannot remain in a dusty place like this. So, if possible, avoid the risk."

As there was no other way out, Pastor Mathews returned to Udaipur in the first week of July. His condition worsened after reaching Udaipur. He was admitted in the Medical College. Pastor did not allow anyone to pass this information onto Mary who was still at Navapur. However, their second daughter Glory called Mary and apprised her of the situation. Mary wanted to be at her husband's side as soon as she could. But Pastor Mathews forbade her to return, giving up the ministries they had been involved in at Navapur at the half-way mark. "If Marykutty comes here, I will go to Navapur." This threat worked. Mary continued to do the Gospel work at Navapur.

# 20

# PASSING THE BATON

Pastor Mathews reached Navapur two days prior to the convention in November. That year's convention had a speciality about it. It was the Silver Jubilee convention of the Filadelfia Church. Pastor Mathews returned to Udaipur on the concluding Sunday of the convention while Mary stayed back in Navapur, taking care of the remaining work.

The following Friday, Pastor Mathews called Mary on the phone and told her:

"While you are there, you must identify the villages which are without any evangelist and where God's work is most needed. A pastor of the Team Mission is in Nandurbar. His name is Gladwin. Discuss this with him. Let us find out the places without any work and start ministries in those places. "

The next day itself, Mary went to Pastor Gladwin and discussed matters with him. While she got up to leave, Pastor Gladwin handed over a tie, a pair of socks, and five hundred rupees in a cover and told her, "Please, give this to Pastor Mathews. He is my spiritual teacher."

While she was returning through Navapur town, she met the shopkeeper who had given provisions needed for the convention on credit.

He asked, "Madam, haven't you gone back to Udaipur yet?"

"How can I go back, when we owe you money for the provisions we bought on credit from you?" Mary replied laughing.

Upon hearing her reply, the shopkeeper said, "We don't even have the slightest fear about the money you owe us. There is no need to stay back here for that. You can payback whenever you have the cash in hand."

Mary mentioned to Pastor Mathews, about the conversation she had with the shopkeeper that day. Pastor Mathews was elated and said, "if it is so", you come back."

After holding a small get together with snacks for the brethren of Karanji Khurd who had put in so much hard work behind the convention, Mary set out for Udaipur again on a Sunday evening.

A few days ago, Pastor Mathews had received a phone call from a person in Bangalore. This person had never met either Pastor Mathews or Mary. But on the phone, he gave a message for Pastor Mathews. "I am about to give you rest. But your wife will have to run harder than she has ever done before. In fact, she will have to run like a man and take care of the ministry."

Pastor Mathews called Mary and told her about this. Both of them laughed and thought that this was just a reminder that they had to work harder in the days to come. But there was a secret message in that prophecy that would only be revealed in the days to come.

Mary was on her way to Udaipur. It was only after reaching Udaipur that she came to know about the journey that Pastor Mathews was about to make to Amritsar in Punjab to speak in a leader's conference there. Suddenly, a disturbing memory rushed into Mary's mind. Ten or twelve years ago, they both had gone to preach in a meeting in Punjab and there Pastor Mathews had come under a severe attack of asthma. But, Mary did not share that unpleasant memory with her husband; she suppressed it in her mind.

Mary was extremely reluctant to send him alone for she knew that he was not in good health, and neither did he enjoy travelling alone. But, on the journey to Amritsar, he was unable to take her along, despite her wish to accompany him. The reason being that the flight ticket to Delhi and the train ticket from there to Amritsar were already provided by the organisation that had invited him for the conference. If he had to take Mary along it would mean a lot of cancellations. As he did not want to make this rearrangement, he had no other option but to leave Mary behind.

The flight to Delhi from Udaipur was scheduled at 3 p.m in the afternoon. At about 1.30 pm, Pastor Mathews left home for the airport after prayer. When he emerged from his house, his family, Bible college teachers, students and others were standing outside. He bid farewell to all of them amidst fun and hearty laughter. Then, he went to the airport.

After reaching Delhi, he called up brother Abraham P. Ninan, the accountant of the Filadelfia ministries in Udaipur, and told him, "I left without giving any money in Mary's hand. Make sure you give two thousand rupees to her."

He was to rest there in Delhi that day and catch the train to Amritsar the next morning. He dined with the hosts in the house where he was staying and later sat chatting with them for some time. After making a request to wake him up as early as possible in the morning, he retired to his room.

Early in the morning, the hosts knocked on the door and called him. But, there was no response. Thinking that he might be sleeping sound, they knocked repeatedly. When there was no response at all even after knocking for a long time, they felt anxious and called on Pastor Mathews' mobile phone. They called many times, but he was not picking up their calls.

A song about Christian hope in Malayalam language, the ring tone on his phone, repeated itself whenever they called.

When all their attempts to wake him up became futile, they peeped through the window on the other side of the room. Pastor Mathews was lying on the bed covered up to his neck, with only his face visible.

Pastor Mathews had the habit of getting up in the wee hours of the morning i.e. around 2.30 or 3 am. Perhaps, he might have woken up early morning that day as well. At that time he might have sensed something. The realization that he was going to depart from this world might have sunk in because normally, he did not like to cover himself. But, in his last sleep he had covered himself well against his habit.

Pastor Mathews had bidden farewell to this world after finishing his race in the 61st year of his life. The global Christian community was shocked to hear the news.

Udaipur was literally shaken by the news of Pastor Mathews' demise. People inside the Filadelfia family and outside could not be controlled.

However, Mary had not yet come to know about the death of her beloved husband. Everyone intentionally hid it from her. In fact, nobody had the courage to convey the sad news to her.

She heard from the Bible College students that her son Paul and daughter-in-law Christy were crying at their residence upstairs. When Mary went up there she saw that all those gathered there had wet eyes, but she could not get any indication as to why they were crying. She also became a bit annoyed with all of them as she felt that they were trying to hide something from her.

Finally, her son-in-law Dr. Finny Philip broke the news to her. They all had feared that she would react strongly to the sad news. But, Mary did not react in an uncontrollable manner. She did not even cry loudly. She seemed to be filled with a heavenly hope. Perhaps, it was because of her unfathomable hope and faith in Christ that when told about Pastor Mathews' home-going, she responded saying: "Can we go to Delhi and pray for resurrecting him?"

Mary might have responded thus because of the feeling that there were many more promises of God that were yet to be fulfilled. The funeral was held on Sunday, 27th November, 2005. It was one of the most attended funerals in the history of Udaipur. From ordinary people to prominent persons belonging to socio-political and cultural scenario, all had come to pay their last homage to him.

# 21

# THE NEXT STAGE

**M**ary could not come to terms with the reality of her husband's departure from this world. As he used to travel constantly for the Lord's work, often she would feel that he had gone somewhere far and would come back as usual laughing and sharing jokes. But, often the reality stung and she felt its sharp pain.

She saw a vision which removed her agony, sadness and emptiness from her heart. It became another turning point in her life. She saw that great vision on the morning of Saturday, the 31st of November.

Pastor Mathews was standing in her room with a beaming face! In the vision, Mary asked her husband, "How can you smile after fooling everyone?"

The Pastor replied, still smiling wide, "Weren't you beside me when I was writing the interpretation to the Book of Revelation, *Revelation Simplified: Glimpses of Eternity*? Don't you remember Mary that I had written about eternity, heaven and other allied matters in that book? Do you know this? Actually, heaven is many times more beautiful than its description in that book! Why are you all crying because I have come to such great a place? You should feel happy."

After saying that, Pastor Mathews gradually faded away from that vision. Mary opened her eyes as if from dream to reality. After the revelation of the vision, Mary never again felt sad or dejected over the death of her husband as a heavenly hope permeated her soul.

The tiny girl of yore who had staggered and strayed from her faith when she lost her mother at the age of ten has now come a long way since that tormenting phase of her childhood. She has now covered a great deal of distance travelling steadily the path of faith! She had her ups and downs, but nothing could distract or detach her from the love of Christ!

The scripture verses quoted below are a mirror held against the life of Mary:

"Who shall separate us from the love of Christ? Shall trouble or hardship or persecution or famine or nakedness or danger or sword?" "No, in all these things we are more than conquerors through him who loved us. For I am convinced that neither death nor life, neither angels nor demons, neither the present nor the future, nor any powers, neither height nor depth, nor anything else in all creation, will be able to separate us from the love of God that is in Christ Jesus our Lord." (Romans 8: 35, 37-39)

In a country like India at a time when no one had even begun to think of sending girls to Bible schools, Mary went to a Bible school defying strong objections from all quarters, even when she had passed out of high school with flying colours!

Since her childhood, Mary has not been walking on paths paved by someone else; on the other hand, paths have formed wherever she has walked.

## Chapter 21

At a time when there was no conveyance and development, Mary travelled across North India, in buses, on foot, in bicycles, in bullock carts, in a manner that could surprise even men, planting churches and grooming evangelists. Her missionary life comes as an inspiration to every woman who has a desire to do something for God.

It seems that there aren't many women in the history of evangelism in India like Mary, who can be presented as a role model for women to emulate.

Indeed God has raised her up for such a time as this.

Let this book cause you to take up the glorious task of spreading the good-news at any cost and also to raise up people who will go out with a burden to reach the lost.

# NOT JUST A WOMAN
# BUT A WOMAN OF FAITH:
### Excerpts from an interview with Mrs. Mary Mathews:

Mrs. Mary Mathews, the co-founder of the Native Missionary Movement and its associate ministries, has been in this exciting journey for long and has seen the goodness of the Lord in myriad ways. Fondly called 'Mary Aunty', she is a mother not just for her three children, but for thousands of others too. She spends her time travelling to the mission fields, encouraging believers and families at home, writing and correcting books. She enjoys cooking and serving and also spending time with her grandchildren.

Following is an excerpt from an interview by Pastor Benny Varghese with Mrs. Mary Mathews:

Q: **You faced separation from your mother at the age of 10, saw uncertain days as a young girl, went on to study in a Bible College, married a missionary and then began your journey to an unknown land. How do you feel now when you look back at the events of your life?**

A: Many times we fail to understand why we face tough days and pain in our lives. But God has a purpose behind allowing us to undergo these experiences whether big or small, good or bad, bitter or sweet. Through the painful experiences of my life, I realized that God has been shaping me and forming me into His own image. Every challenge is an opportunity for a higher purpose.

Q: **Have you had frustration due to unfulfilled desires in your life or ministry? How have you got out of it?**

A: There has never been any unfulfilled desire in my life. I have never given too much priority to fulfilling my own desires. Fulfilling God's desire has always been my heart's desire. Disappointments have come in my life. But I have always depended on the Word of God to overcome such disappointments. I read the Bible every time I became disappointed. While spending time reading my Bible, I have felt God speaking to me. Since the days of my youth, God's word has been very close to my heart. It is only God's word that has sustained me in my life.

**Q: What has been the biggest trial that you have faced in your life? How did God help you to overcome it?**

**A:** The unexpected separation from my husband has been the biggest trial of my life. In the beginning, I could not believe when I heard the news of his death. Even today, after eight years, I sometimes find it hard to accept the fact that my husband is no more with me. His separation created a big emptiness in my life. But God's presence filled my loneliness and emptiness, comforted me and led me in His way. The painful experiences of my life taught me some lessons of life which I would like to share with you.

First, we need to always be prepared in life to face challenges. Anything can happen at any time.

Second, if we desire to do something for God or man, do it as fast as possible, because time will run out.

Third, God's presence is the only presence that will never leave us. Anybody can get separated from us or we could be separated from them at any time.

Even though I knew all these things, they were just knowledge for me. But after the separation from my husband they have become my life's experience.

Now, even when I have to travel alone to places, I don't find it difficult since I know that God has a purpose and His presence is always with me.

**Q: Can you tell me the names of some people who have inspired you the most?**

**A:** More than people, the stories of the lives of missionaries have greatly inspired me. For instance, the life of the American missionary Jim Elliot (1927 - 1956) has deeply touched me. He was killed in Ecuador, during their evangelization program among the Auca tribe that lived in the rainforest of that country. The challenges faced by missionary families, and the way in which they have withstood tough times of their life has always strengthened me and given me the courage to look to my God and to move forward in life.

**Q: Which verse in the Bible has deeply touched you?**

**A:** "And we know that all things work together for good to those who love God, to those who are the called according to His purpose." Romans 8:28.

The Word of God is powerful and timely but at times when I've felt that my prayers were not being answered, in the midst of confusions of life, this Word has greatly encouraged and held me.

**Q: What are some of the things that you would like to see when there is revival in the church?**

**A:** We are praying for revival and it will take place but it can only happen when the lives of people are changed from within. There is a deep cry and thirst in every believer to become more like Jesus. Though it's not easy but it is my prayer that our church would be revived and every believer would become more like Jesus with each passing day.

**Q: What are some of the special qualities you have seen in Dr. Thomas Mathews?**

**A:** If I say in one word, he was a man of faith. But still let me number his qualities:

- Whatever the Bible says he believed as it is.
- The verse "Rejoice in the Lord always, again I say rejoice" in the epistle to the Philippians; I was always able to see the depth and meaning of this verse in him.
- He would underline even those verses in his Bible, which a small child used while preaching a message.
- Humility and politeness were an integral part of his personality.
- Intense reading was one of his special qualities.
- He was a person who would pray in the time of need.
- His passion to reach the unreached has led thousands to Christ.

Let me finish by saying that in every sense he has lived an exemplary life.

**Q: What is your message for our sisters in Christ?**

**A:** There are several things that I want to share with our sisters today. Some of them are:

- "Whatever has been said in the Word of God is true. The verses in the Word of God are not meant only for men, but, for women as well. When the Holy Spirit works, not only men, but women are empowered too."

- "Any woman who wants to be used for the Kingdom of God should not consider her circumstances. You may be a housewife or a working woman, but, God can use you in your existing state."

- "In the absence of the fullness of the Holy Spirit and without a burden for the perishing souls of the world, a woman may not succeed even if she claims to be in full-time ministry."

- "To have a family and raise children is a real blessing. But, then the first priority should always be accorded to God and the kingdom of God. The children too are to be raised up with this thought."

- "Life becomes meaningful only when the purposes of God are understood."

- "Wherever we are, the Kingdom of God and His righteousness should be revealed through us, there. When we say Kingdom and righteousness, all blessings of God, are included in it. That means protection is from God, peace is from God and authority is from God! When all these add up together a woman will not mark herself down saying, "I am just a woman." Instead, she will lift herself up. The reason is simple. A woman who has gained the vibrant energy of God is not just a woman. She is much more than that!"

**Q: What are the dreams that you would like to see come true?**

**A:** My dream is that there should be churches planted in all the areas of north India. I am praying that each *taluka* (an administrative district comprising of a number of villages) must have at-least one church. A lot of Christian literature in the Hindi language must be made available so that the churches are well groomed. This literature should reach every person's hand, especially young men and women. These have been my major all-time desires and dreams.

*Last Picture of Dr. Thomas Mathews with his family*

# REFERENCES

- *Marubhoomiyil Thalarathe* (Tireless in the Desert)
  by Thomas Kaithamangalam - Malayalam

- *Marubhoomiyile Apposthalan* (The Apostle in the Desert)
  by Thomas Thonnakkal - Malayalam

- *He Saw a Man Named Mathews* by John Thollander - English

- *Vision, Mission and Movement* by Roger Simmons - English